GENDER AND HEROISM

IN EARLY

ENGLISH LITERATURE

Mart
Tel:

To

Gender and Heroism in Early Modern English Literature

Mary Beth Rose

THE UNIVERSITY OF CHICAGO PRESS
Chicago & London

Mary Beth Rose is professor of English and director of the Institute for the Humanities at the University of Illinois at Chicago. She is coeditor of *Elizabeth I: Collected Works* and the author of *The Expense of Spirit: Love and Sexuality in English Renaissance Drama.*

The University of Chicago Press, Chicago 60637
The University of Chicago Press, Ltd., London
© 2002 by The University of Chicago
All rights reserved. Published 2002
Printed in the United States of America

11   10   09   08   07   06   05   04   03   02   1   2   3   4   5
ISBN: 0-226-72572-3 (cloth)
ISBN: 0-226-72573-1 (paper)

Library of Congress Cataloging-in-Publication Data

Rose, Mary Beth.
    Gender and heroism in early modern English literature / Mary Beth Rose.
        p.   cm.
    Includes bibliographical references and index.
    ISBN 0-226-72572-3 (alk. paper) — ISBN 0-226-72573-1 (pbk. : alk. paper)
    1. English literature—Early modern, 1500–1700—History and
criticism.   2. Courage in literature.   3. Women and literature—Great
Britain—History—16th century.   4. Women and literature—Great
Britain—History—17th century.   5. Women—Great Britain—
Biography—History and criticism.   6. Sex role in literature.
7. Heroines in literature.   8. Patience in literature.   9. Heroes in
literature.   I. Title.
    PR428.C638 R67   2002
    820.9′353—dc21   2001048008

♾ The paper used in this publication meets the minimum requirements of the American National Standard for Information Sciences—Permanence of Paper for Printed Library Materials, ANSI Z39.48-1992.

For Nick
and in memory of Uncle Don

Contents

Acknowledgments

❁My greatest intellectual debts are to Frances Dolan, Margaret Ferguson, Jean Howard, and Teresa Toulouse. Without their imaginative engagement and suggestions, this book would be very different. Without their friendship, it probably would not exist. I cannot ever thank them enough.

For attentive and sympathetic reading of all or part of the material, I am grateful to Michael Lieb, Leah Marcus, Leonard Barkan, Valerie Traub, Natalie Zemon Davis, and Albert Labriola. I have had the fortunate opportunity to work with Alan Thomas of the University of Chicago Press. His insights and talents as an editor would benefit any book. I thank Jenni L. Fry for her thoughtful copyediting. Working with Randolph Petilos at the Press is also a pleasure.

I am grateful to the American Council of Learned Societies for the fellowship that allowed me to complete the book. I thank audiences at lectures I gave at Florida State, St. Louis, Harvard, Louisiana State, Illinois State, and Columbia Universities, as well as the Universities of Alabama, Akron, Colorado at Boulder, Massachusetts, and Mississippi, for the helpful questions and insights they offered while I was developing this project. A very brief summary of chapter 2 appeared in *PMLA* 115, no. 5 (October 2000). © 2000 by The Modern Language Association of America. All rights reserved. Reprinted by permission of the Modern Language Association. Chapter 3 is a much-revised version of an essay from *Women in the Middle Ages and the Renaissance: Literary and Historical Perspectives,* a book I edited that was published by Syracuse University Press in 1986. Chapter 4 is a slightly altered version of an essay by the same title that appeared in *Milton Studies* 33 (The Miltonic Samson), Albert C. Labriola and Michael Lieb, guest editors, © 1997. Reprinted by permission of the University of Pittsburgh Press. I thank all these publications for permission to reprint material. Throughout the book, in many cases spelling in quotations from early modern sources has been silently modernized.

ℭDuring the years I spent writing this study of heroism, I had unending personal support from Denny Luria, Jeff Berg, Kate Berg, Lily Berg, Roslyn Lieb, and Mary Pat Mauro. I trust they know how glad I am for their friendship. The book is dedicated to my one and only wonderful nephew, Nicholas Rose Flores, and to the memory of my uncle, Don McGuire, who rooted for all my efforts and probably never suspected how much his disciplined commitment to work helped me.

Prologue

☙For most readers or spectators, the idea of the heroic calls to mind socially or morally elevated protagonists waging war and managing politics: courageous, superior, noteworthy individuals creating or redefining the public sphere. The stress on movement and adventure, on rescue, rule, exploration, and conquest, points to a tradition of heroism as distinctively masculine. The notion of heroism as idealized, public, male action suits with precision the narrative convincingly established by recent scholarship examining early modern politics, law, medicine, philosophy, and economic and social history in relation to gender. This narrative posits a long process in which public and private spheres become increasingly separate, with consolidating boundaries explicitly defined as distinct. In a corresponding movement, the public sphere becomes (in powerful concept if not in actual fact) almost completely masculine. Women—or cultural conceptions of the female—are excluded from the questing, striving, and conquering that both form the heroic subject and characterize his actions; with accelerating modernization, what is female becomes increasingly confined to a domestic—and so, it is argued, devalued—private world.[1]

Recently this narrative has been challenged by those who question the assumption that women enjoyed a higher status before the advent of capitalism and industrialization, as well as by scholars primarily concerned with material practices, which inevitably fail to correspond with prescriptive codes of conduct. However it has been nuanced and complicated, though, the argument that early modern England experienced the beginnings of a more defined public-private division that clearly separates the genders, conflating what is masculine with what is public, becomes enriched rather than weakened. Even when detached from issues of progress or its lack, or considered in terms of the blurred boundaries between continuity and change, the larger trajectory of the argument remains intact.[2]

Yet the gendering of heroism from the late sixteenth to the late seventeenth centuries in England does not reveal an accelerating idealization of that which is male, public, and active, but rather the opposite. Indeed, an exclusive focus on these qualities obscures a more passive but equally potent dimension of heroic identity that by the late seventeenth century emerges as dominant: that which privileges not the active confrontation with danger, but the capacity to endure it, to resist and suffer with patience and fortitude, rather than to confront and conquer with strength and wit. "Thou hast not half the power to do me harm / As I have to be hurt," Emilia declares triumphantly to Othello (5.2.163–64); or, as Milton puts it in a less defiantly victimized but equally self-assured line in his sonnet on his blindness, "They also serve who only stand and wait" (19.14).[3] Rather than acts of killing and conquest, the patient suffering of error, misfortune, disaster, and malevolence is idealized in a newly and self-consciously constructed heroism of endurance that privileges the private life and pointedly rejects war. One need only think of *Paradise Lost,* in which the arena for human heroism is neither war nor politics, but marriage.

Focusing on texts that range from the late sixteenth to the late seventeenth centuries in England, this book explores processes of change in the representation of heroism. The central historical argument—by which I mean the argument about change over time—contends that during the early modern period the claims of both active and passive heroism are intensely scrutinized, and that eventually the heroism of endurance takes precedence over the heroics of action. Why do these developments take place? As noted, the prestige granted the heroics of endurance at the end of the seventeenth century, privileging privacy and passive suffering, seems to contradict the very convincing narrative that separates gendered spheres and idealizes public action which is almost exclusively male. Yet the reasons for changing representations of heroism are clarified when viewed as part of, rather than as running counter to, the larger cultural effort to distinguish and distinctly gender private and public spheres.

This cultural work is in turn part of the well-documented interconnected processes that accompany the centralization of nation-states in the West. Most important for this analysis are the long and gradual developments that eventually transform both the representation and the enactment of violence. Following Max Weber, Norbert Elias argues that, as the highly differentiated societies of the Middle Ages become regulated states with relatively effective monarchies, the newly formed nation-states achieve "a stable and centralized monopoly of physical violence."[4] Recently scholars have analyzed this phenomenon by focusing on the state's public production of violent punishments—torture and grisly execution—as theatrical, indeed pedagogical, events.[5] But the state's possessive and ostentatious assumption of its terrifying new powers also has direct consequences for representations of heroism. In particular it renders anachronistic the idealized figure of the independent, aristocratic male warrior who, protecting himself and his dependents, excels at individual, hand-to-hand combat. Michael Murrin has exhaustively demonstrated the technological changes in warfare and weaponry and the rise of standing armies that contribute to the decline of the individual knight-warrior's heroic status.[6] The male warrior of course endures as a heroic figure in Renaissance literature, but his status becomes ever more residual, like the chivalric imagery that adorns the Elizabethan court. He seems to exist either to celebrate the lost past (Henry V, Spenser's knights) or to mourn it (Castiglione's courtier, Antony, Edgar, the aged Lear himself). As scrutiny of traditional heroism and of aristocracy becomes more pointed and intense, the male warrior becomes less of an elegiac and more of a problematic figure. He is an upstart renegade (Tamburlaine), a madman (Hieronimo, Hamlet, Ferdinand), a criminal (Richard III, Macbeth); or, in a mysterious correspondence, his outsized military ability coexists with a helpless inadequacy in the face of civilian social demands (Coriolanus), particularly those of private life (Othello).

In addition to cultural changes directly involving violent conquest, scholars have thoroughly documented the processes of upward and downward social mobility that characterize English culture during and after the Protestant Reformation. These processes include the increasing commercialization and move to money economies that give new prominence to a class of men who rise as courtiers, merchants, and bureaucrats through education and through intellectual, diplomatic, and financial achievement, rather than securing origin and birth through individual—or at least decentralized—military prowess.[7] Inevitably virtues, desires, and capacities more germane to these middle-class cultural endeavors than to aristocratic valor, largesse, and entitlement begin to be idealized. As Elias sums up, "The change in social structure which had long been working against the warrior nobility in favor of bourgeois classes, accelerates in the sixteenth century."[8] Thus existing scholarship that demonstrates the increasing separation and distinctive gendering of public and private spheres, the centralization of the nation-state and accompanying processes of social mobility, the rise of standing armies and the state's monopoly of violence, along with the triumph of Protestantism (about which more below), enables us to locate the transforming representations of heroism in early modern England in a dense and intricate historical context that provides a scenario for change.

My analysis accepts the causal explanations this context offers and builds upon and within them with one significant exception. What has been largely overlooked in arguments that trace the separation of public and private spheres is the significant discursive effort to valorize, rather than trivialize, private life: in short, to make the private sphere heroic. In England this effort can be related directly to the triumph of Protestantism, with its emphasis on interiority and the capacities and obligations of the individual self: as Elias puts it, "[T]he battlefield is moved within."[9] I have argued at length elsewhere that, when English Protestant reformers construct a new idealization of marriage in the sixteenth and seventeenth centuries, they represent marriage as an epic endeavor and describe its undertaking in military terms common to the male heroics of action. Marriage becomes "this one and absolutely greatest action of a man's whole life," requiring unwavering commitment and assuming the properties of inevitable destiny: "as thereon depending the future good or evil of a man's whole aftertime and days." It provides the arena where an individual can struggle and meet death or defeat, triumph or salvation: "for marriage is an adventure, for whosoever marries, adventures; he adventures his peace, his freedom, his liberty, his body; yea, and sometimes his soul too." Marriage is a perilous odyssey, a voyage on a dangerous sea, "wherein so many shipwreck for want of better knowledge and advice upon a rock."[10]

What are the strategies necessary for the successful hero of marriage? "It is in this action as in a strategem of war"[11]; "a valiant soldier doth never repent of the battle, because he meets with strong enemies; he resolves to be a conqueror, and then the more and stronger his foes, the greater his honour"[12]; "[domestic] authority is like a sword."[13]

Nevertheless the initiating destructive energy needed in war has some disadvantages in the marital battle: "A wise, grave, peaceable man may always have his sword in readiness, and that also very bright, keen, and sharp: but he will not be very ready to pluck it out of his scabberd."[14] Like the virtues emerging as crucial to success in early modern economic and political affairs, those required by the heroics of marriage turn out not to be the equivalent of those that guarantee the violent domination achieved by the heroics of action. Although deploying metaphors of violence to establish its prestige and importance, marital heroism instead depends upon chastity, humility, obedience, and the patient suffering of affliction. "So must the husband and wife resolve to conquer the troubles of marriage, and use the buckler of patience against the blows of adversity, that they may conquer," exhorts William Whately.[15] While demanding courage equal to the heroics of action, the heroism of marriage requires not direct aggression, but self-sacrifice and endurance.

Early modern Western culture reveals an ongoing preoccupation with both the male heroics of action and the heroics of endurance.[16] With its multiplicity of sources, including Seneca and the stoics, the lives of the Catholic saints, the continuing popularity of medieval treatises on the art of dying, Patient Griselda stories, and the careers and tribulations of both Protestant and Jesuit martyrs related to Renaissance audiences, the heroics of endurance is not so clearly gendered as the heroics of action, and includes both sexes among its protagonists. Nevertheless it is striking that the terms which constitute the heroics of endurance are precisely those terms used to construct the early modern idealization of women: patient suffering, mildness, humility, chastity, loyalty, and obedience. Contending that the heroics of endurance ultimately takes precedence over the heroics of action, I am also claiming that, by the end of the seventeenth century, the terms in which heroism is constructed and performed as the endurance of suffering are predominantly gendered female.

The heroes discussed in this book are both men and women, male and female. In my use of the terms "male" and "female" I situate myself within recent theoretical discussions that, exploring the discursive con-structedness of gender, recognize that subject positions labeled "fe-male" and "male" are not necessarily inhabited in that order by female and male protagonists in texts or by actual, embodied women and men. Rather these gendered terms refer to normative positions, created in language and idealized repeatedly in multiple discursive domains in the Renaissance. Thus men can occupy female subject positions and vice versa; but when men, for example, do inhabit female positions, their doing so is valued differently from women's occupying similar struc-tural positions. As I show in chapter 1, when Marlowe's Tamburlaine abducts and rapes his wife-to-be, audience or readers might see her as victim and object; but when Tamburlaine represents himself as a raped woman, Marlowe presents this self-characterization as an instance of Tamburlaine's commanding, persuasive magnetism. Similarly, when Ben Jonson's Volpone chooses to occupy silent and passive positions, the audience is meant to view him not as subordinate, marginalized, and subdued, but as witty, strategic, outrageous, and shrewd.

In *Bodies That Matter* Judith Butler clarifies her notion of gender as performative by stressing performance not as a limitlessly theatrical ac-tivity but as a "reiteration of norms or a set of norms." She describes this process as "citational": the citing of conventions of authority constitutes and reconstitutes that authority through repetition. Social construc-tivism, Butler argues, "needs to take account of the domain of con-straints without which a certain living and desiring being cannot make its way." Although delimiting, constructed norms are necessary for an intelligible life in culture; gender is the "social significance that sex as-sumes within a given culture." Subject to such definitional formulations and articulated in their terms, the performance of gender is neverthe-less not wholly determined and constrained. Butler stresses that regu-latory schema are "historically revisable criteria of intelligibility which produce and vanquish bodies that matter." Furthermore, no matter how tenaciously normative positions are cited and reiterated, there is always that which escapes their definitional power: "the instability produced by the effort to fix the site of the sexed body challenges the boundaries of discursive intelligibility."[17]

The last twenty years or so of research have revealed a normative economy of gender in the Renaissance based on hierarchy—the male is superior and commanding, the female inferior and subordinate—and on binary opposition—his unity and coherence clarify her dispersal and fragmentation; his identification with the soul underscores and transcends hers with the body; his mobility demands her stasis; his speech is animated by her silence. Simply viewed, these connective chains become embodied in representation by active male subjects and passive female objects. Whatever their differences, contradictions, evasions, and slippages, legal, political, scientific, religious, and domestic discourses all base the gendered subject positions they prescribe as normative on the assumed superiority of that which is male. Relevant discourses construct aristocratic male positions as political leaders, warriors, sportsmen, and poets; while the aristocratic female, even when educated and accomplished, must serve primarily as the inspiration of masculine endeavor and the provider of (preferably male) heirs through whom property is legitimized and transmitted. Similarly, in the more middle-class households, domesticity is seen to depend upon the male as the public figure, provider, and determiner of meaning, linked to the female as wife, sister, and mother, ideally characterized by her chastity, silence, and obedience. To quote Daniel Boyarin, actual lived lives may not have followed these models, "but the models themselves are a significant cultural fact."[18] The gendered economy that results from them envisages women as having symbolic power rather than direct agency, influence rather than control. As Renaissance literature repeatedly makes clear, any woman who insists on maintaining autonomous agency is (often violently) doomed.[19]

In the four chronologically arranged chapters that follow, I examine the ways in which normative gendered positions assume heroic proportions in early modern English literature as they are diversely modified, celebrated, undermined, scrutinized, and obscured. The basic premise of my analysis is that heroism is part of a process in which a culture

assigns meanings and determines values. A traditional, indeed pre-
dominant view equates heroism with conflict, struggle, and personal
courage: that is, with a kind of behavior, psychology, or morality. Students, for example, when asked to define a hero, invariably invoke a
figure who is independent and risk-taking, stronger than others, often
self-sacrificing and bravely refusing to compromise, fighting for what he
or she believes. In contrast, I begin by considering heroic identity
abstractly, as a position in a textual structure that can be filled by individual, gendered agents. Specifically, I view the heroic as a gendered positioning of the self in relation to pleasure and power. I argue that the
heroic position articulates the central significances—the confluence of
meanings—in a text. What elements of human action and identity are
being highlighted, stressed, idealized, and privileged; which are de-
emphasized, marginalized, or excluded in the representation of heroism? As I will demonstrate, these elements undergo extraordinary re-
arrangement and transformation during the course of the period I
study. By focusing on the role the heroic plays in a culture's assessment
of itself, my analysis presents a narrative of the ways in which literary
representations register and enable changes in value.

The analysis traces transformations of heroism as they are represented in a variety of texts, including plays, poems, autobiographies,
political speeches, a novel, and religious and moral tracts concerned
with defining gender. While considering texts that range over a century
of English literature, I do not attempt to be comprehensive. Instead I
undertake a mode of reading that focuses on case studies, on selected
genres and subjects as these manifest themselves at particular moments. Readers may feel frustrated at the omission of seemingly obvious texts: The Faerie Queene, for example, or Hamlet; the heroic drama of
the later seventeenth century, or Paradise Lost. Focusing on the drama of
the 1630s could reveal the ways in which changes in manners begin to
privilege the virtues of more bourgeois heroes. A discussion of Christ's
heroism as female in Paradise Regained, to cite another example, would
augment the historical argument about the ways in which heroic representation has changed by the end of the seventeenth century. Indeed,
every time I have given various parts of this book as lectures, people

have made helpful suggestions about other examples to include, several of which I have already listed. In the end I decided against greater inclusiveness because, while a wider array of texts would have added weight to my analysis, it would not have altered the central historical argument about the changing trajectory of heroic representation in early modern England.

The rationale for the selection of texts has to do with my desire to create a new perspective by shedding a different kind of light on standard texts, as I do in the first chapter; examining relatively new or noncanonical material, as I do in the second and third chapters; and linking analytically texts usually thought to have little in common, as I do in chapter 4. Chapter 1 addresses the question of what happens to the female in the construction and performance of a male heroism of action. I examine this issue in four plays that are predominantly preoccupied with heroic masculinity: Marlowe's *Tamburlaine* and *Dr. Faustus*; Ben Jonson's *Volpone*; and Shakespeare's *Macbeth*.

It is often assumed that female positions either are excluded from the heroism of action or, when deemed advantageous or strong, are appropriated both conceptually and in fact by the inevitable dominance of that which is male. The female simply is not present, or only indirectly important, in the performance of active heroism. While not questioning the accuracy of this narrative of the containment of the female, I do want to complicate it. Examining the ways in which Tamburlaine, Faustus, and Volpone position themselves structurally in their quests for pleasure and power, I argue that women, or the female, are neither simply erased, silenced, nor immobilized, but rather deployed multiply and fluidly by male figures in their performance of heroic identity. In battles, seductions, magic, and shrewd money-making ruses, these hypermasculine characters repeatedly identify themselves with female figures or purposefully occupy passive positions precisely in order to secure their identities. Whether or not it is self-conscious, bad faith enters in the text's (or reader's or viewer's) subsequent refusal to acknowledge this fact in the ways in which prestige and charisma are assigned and perpetuated. The resulting reiteration of norms reveals a reliance on prior positions that stubbornly persists in the face of evidence that undermines those positions: plot and action are renamed in retrospect. To paraphrase Jonathan Goldberg, who writes in a related context, acts are not changed, but only what they are called.[20]

The destabilizing backward move of depending upon the female and then occluding that reliance in the process of constructing the male heroics of action is the focus of the first chapter and remains a theme throughout this book. This process involves more than simple appropriation; although males occupy female positions, masculine domination is neither stable nor successfully sustained. Unlike Tamburlaine, Faustus, and Volpone, Macbeth is one male hero who succeeds in excluding the female from his identity. As I will show, this victory gives his heroism a kind of gendered purity; however, that heroism is represented as criminal and doomed.

The goal of the heroics of action is not limited to the achievement of stable, aristocratic male dominance through violence. Rather the hero's goal is to occupy simultaneously—to monopolize—all dominant gendered subject positions. In so arguing I am situating myself within recent discussions that emphasize the multiplicity of gendered positions that become visible when we stop taking prescriptive norms at face value, assuming their triumph in a variety of cultural domains.[21] In chapter 2 I demonstrate that Elizabeth I is aware of the fluidity of possible gendered positions and exploits it when defining her power in her public speeches.

Much recent scholarship contends that Elizabeth creates herself as *sui generis,* particularly by subsuming her literal female body in a larger symbolic body that is male. Basing my claims in the new edition of Elizabeth's writings, I argue in contrast that she manipulates rhetorically the special prestige of both male and female subject positions without consistently privileging either.[22] Scholars like Maureen Quilligan and Constance Jordan have revealed the rhetorical recourse to lived experience, to sheer bodily existence, as an explicitly female claim to authority that opposes itself to male symbolic systems (e.g., divine right, or the king's two bodies), which for the most part exclude women in sixteenth- and seventeenth-century polemics.[23] My analysis of Elizabeth's public speeches demonstrates that she both opposes and draws on traditional female and traditional male rhetorics of authority when creating her heroic persona.

Survival, with its assumption that existence comprises struggle and achievement, becomes a salient component of female heroic self-creation in the autobiographies of ordinary women, which begin to proliferate in the mid- to the late seventeenth century. In these life accounts, the tension between the relative fluidity of much thinking about gender in the Renaissance and the increasingly well-defined cultural discourses and material practices that systematically consign women to the private sphere is acutely felt. In chapter 3 I examine the life accounts of four Restoration women (Margaret Cavendish, Ann Fanshawe, Anne Halkett, and Alice Thornton) who are neither saints, mystics, nor proselytizers, but traditional, upper-class wives and mothers, all of whom are forced into public action by the English civil war. I argue that the social and political instability generated by the war enabled these traditional women to violate the powerful injunctions against female action and self-expression to which they, consciously at least, adhere. In the lives of women who are not queens, female heroic identity is revealed as by definition contradictory and problematic.

By the end of the seventeenth century, I argue, all heroism becomes problematic and is constituted in terms that are gendered female. I demonstrate how three Restoration texts which form a natural trio but previously have never been read together—Milton's *Samson Agonistes,* Aphra Behn's *Oroonoko,* and Mary Astell's *Some Reflections upon Marriage*—all deconstruct the heroics of action by presenting a sustained critique of physical strength as the basis of male privilege. Beginning with the premise that the heroics of action is ineffectual and anachronistic, all three texts offer an alternative heroics of endurance; and all three focus on compromised agency, or agency inscribed in contradictions, as the defining condition of heroism. In each case this condition is represented in the hero's position of being seduced into slavery.

My own politics and commitments are feminist, and one of the goals of this study is to make visible the ways in which the demonstrable cultural importance of the female in the representation of heroism goes unacknowledged in both the past and the present. My method opens a space in which to integrate discussion of men and women writers. The conception of heroism as the textual location of gendered meanings allows evidence for female heroism, much of which has been invisible, to become legible and articulate. Given these goals, it is important to emphasize that, as the texts discussed in chapter 4 illustrate, the powerful, dominant mode of literary heroism at the end of the seventeenth century is the endurance of suffering, represented in female terms. Further, one can see in the lineaments of this heroism the beginnings of the novel to come.

In addition to its recuperative intentions, my analysis also means to offer a critique of both of the models of heroism I study. That the terms in which heroic meaning is constructed should become female is a process of change that involves its own ironies and complexities, and also its own violence. Rather than the murder or domination beloved by the heroics of action, the heroics of endurance often commends to our attention rape, self-mutilation, solipsistic desire, slavery, and unwanted death. An historical view of transforming representations of the heroic reveals that the adulation of violence is far from being either a present-day phenomenon or limited to one gender.

If, as I have argued, the construction and performance of heroism are processes of cultural evaluation that represent the heroic position as the location in the text that articulates its major significances, then those meanings can appear really grim. In their general outlines the differences between the heroics of action and the heroics of endurance frequently come down to a choice between killing and dying. Given the complexities of human potential, it would seem possible to come up with better options. Even if we grudgingly concede that violence is sometimes necessary, does it have to be idealized and mystified in heroic terms? As I have tried to show, whether or not they are idealized, embedded in both the heroics of action and the heroics of endurance are the human capacity and desire to survive. Given the realities of cultural change, it is at least possible to imagine the representation of that capacity and desire as the most brilliant, the most courageous, the most committed—even the most meaningful—position to be in.

"The observed of all observers": The Gendering of Heroism in Marlowe, Jonson, and Shakespeare

I

I begin with Freud's reflections on heroism, which he explains in terms of audience, or reader, identification: "The feeling of security with which I follow the hero through his dangerous adventures," Freud writes, "is the same as that with which a real hero throws himself into the water to save a drowning man, or exposes himself to the fire of the enemy while storming a battery. It is this very feeling of being a hero which one of our best authors has well expressed in the famous phrase, 'Nothing can happen to me!' It seems to me, however, that this significant mark of invulnerability very clearly betrays—His Majesty the Ego, the hero of all day-dreams and all novels."[1]

Leaving aside the alleged fame of the quoted phrase, Freud's remarks simplify to the point of disregarding the range and complexity of literary endeavor. His allusion to genre, comprehended in a casual reference to the modern novel, ignores the temporality of heroism, or the changing historical conditions that constitute and reconstitute heroic meaning. In his stress on direct, aggressive action, he also overlooks the long and continuing tradition of Western heroism that privileges the passive endurance of suffering. Consequently women—or cultural conceptions of the female—are excluded from the kind of behavior and event that both form the heroic subject and characterize his actions. Freud ironically—and deconstructively—accounts for these actions as the projected, idealizing identifications of the fragile male ego, fantasizing wishfully about its own omnipotence.

Despite the omissions and anachronisms of his description for purposes of literary and historical analysis, Freud's assumption that the heroic is an exclusively masculine province involving—whether or not it is intentional—bad faith in its represented drive toward omnipotence has a real usefulness for exploring Renaissance texts. I, too, want to consider heroic subjectivity as a gendered positioning of the self in relation to pleasure and power and to interrogate this process as unstable. But in what follows I would like to relocate Freud's focus on the individual ego, imagined as transhistorical, to the English Renaissance cultural creation of gender difference, as I investigate the representation of male heroism. How do Renaissance gender norms, themselves idealizations, intersect with the idealizing objectives of active male heroism? Which aspects of gender are being emphasized and which occluded or obscured in the construction of this version of the heroic? How does unraveling that process of evaluation reveal the instabilities of Renaissance heroism as a sustaining and enabling cultural description of masculinity and leadership? To explore these issues, I will focus on *Tamburlaine* and *Dr. Faustus* by Christopher Marlowe and *Volpone* by Ben Jonson; I will turn in comparison and conclusion to Shakespeare's *Macbeth*.

Marlowe and Jonson are playwrights whose seemingly unmitigated masculinism provides a worst (or perhaps for my purposes best) case scenario. Most readers and spectators would agree that each of these dramatists in his different way is as unconcerned with, disgusted by, and eager to marginalize, demonize, and exclude women and the female as it is possible to be and still write plays. And so it appears that the performance of heroic identity in their plays as active and phallic in the extreme (that is, gendered exclusively male) is constructed and dependent upon marginalizing and erasing—optimally completely excluding—the female. In what follows it is certainly not my wish to deny the intent to contain the female in Marlowe's and Jonson's versions of male heroism. But what I find more interesting is that the attempt proves unsuccessful and, indeed, impossible. I will argue that in *Tamburlaine, Dr. Faustus,* and *Volpone,* female positions are neither simply erased, silenced, nor immobilized, but rather inhabited flexibly and with desire in the performance of heroic identity by male figures. I will show that the active male hero's quest for omnipotence as exemplified in these texts does not seek to achieve the undiluted triumph of a dominant masculinity, but rather to monopolize all gendered subject positions.

The bad faith in this construction of heroism therefore inheres in its nominal and subsequent privileging of maleness; because femaleness is not merely included in this form of heroic identity as Marlowe and Jonson construct it, but is demonstrably constituent of that identity.

In contrast, it is Shakespeare's Macbeth who keeps the faith with the gendering of male heroism as it is idealized in Renaissance texts. Macbeth's quest to conquer and dominate takes the unambiguous form of eliminating women and the female. His journey is a savage one; but within the logic of male tragic heroism, it is supremely successful. In contrast to Tamburlaine's, Faustus's, and Volpone's, Macbeth's heroic identity is at once more idealistic, more terrifying, and more pristine. Because of the gendered purity of the hero's quest, *Macbeth* provides the most unrelenting scrutiny and scathing critique of aristocratic male heroism in all of English Renaissance literature.

II

Marlowe's *Tamburlaine,* parts 1 and 2 (1587–88), provides a case in point—perhaps *the* case in point—for the privileging of active male agency in defining and achieving heroic dominance. Creating himself through words and deeds, persuading, punishing, conquering, commanding, Tamburlaine is the man "ordained by heaven / To further every action to the best" (1.2.1.52–53).[2] Living out his fantasies and obsessions linguistically, he brazenly colonizes the imperative mood, for as he puts it, "*will* and *shall* best fitteth Tamburlaine" (1.3.3.41). The famous speeches in the play all emphasize Tamburlaine's heroic identity as rooted in a desire for omnipotence, idealized as courageous, nearly successful striving actually to fulfill human potential:

> Nature that framed us of four elements,
> Warring within our breasts for regiment,
> Doth teach us all to have aspiring minds:
> Our souls, whose faculties can comprehend
> The wondrous architecture of the world,
> And measure every wandering planet's course,
> Still climbing after knowledge infinite,
> And always moving as the restless spheres,
> Wills us to wear ourselves and never rest.
> (1.2.7.18–26)

Soul-driven, desiring, and questing, Tamburlaine is self-consciously constructed as the male hero of action par excellence. His relationship with his abducted victim turned concubine turned wife, Zenocrate, whom he first degrades and then idealizes, augments and elaborates the paradigmatic quality of his heroic performance. Tamburlaine's only moment of conflict in part 1 is construed, again paradigmatically, as an unresolved struggle between love and duty, arising when Zenocrate begs him to refrain from savaging her country and murdering her father, which he has sworn to do. He does, in fact, partly give in to her by keeping her father alive, acknowledging that "neither Persia's sovereign nor the Turk / Troubled my senses with conceit of foil / So much by much as doth Zenocrate" (1.5.1.157–59). In his love for Zenocrate Tamburlaine recognizes the dangerous potential for the defeat of his military ambitions. His defensive reaction is to abstract from the immediate and personal: "What is beauty, saith my sufferings then?" he ponders philosophically (1.5.1.160). Rejecting his feelings as "unseemly," "effeminate," and "faint," by the end of this soliloquy he has articulated eloquently the traditional Neoplatonic / Petrarchan chivalric solution to the dilemma of male heterosexual desire in its relation to action. The beloved lady (subsumed here as an embodied presence by abstracted musing) must be internalized as an image, serving as the inspiration for Tamburlaine's military conquests: "And every warrior that is rapt with love / Of fame, of valor, and of victory, / Must needs have beauty beat on his conceits" (1.5.1.180–82). Repressing, or from his point of view transcending, sexual desire, Tamburlaine is able to conclude his soliloquy by returning to the theme of military glory, now psychologically unimpeded.

Along with inspiring Tamburlaine, Zenocrate's function in the play is to add a moral dimension completely absent in the hero himself that at least partially qualifies his magnificence. Yet, as I have argued at length elsewhere, Zenocrate as embodied presence has little meaningful agency. Because she occupies a static and decorative role for the majority of the play, it is appropriate that Zenocrate's final appearance in part 2 is as a portrait decorating the coffin that contains her corpse. Despite Zenocrate's elevation of the play's moral tone, her narrative role is destructive. She fulfills her woman's part, which, from the point of view of dramatic structure, can be seen to impede the progress of masculine heroics. Through the devastating effect her death has on Tamburlaine, she can also be said to provide the prologue to the hero's doom.[3]

The story of Tamburlaine and Zenocrate presents the familiar plot of the masterful male, constructing a heroism based on military conquest, political command, and possession of the conquered female, who is internalized as image, objectified, indeed fetishized, for these purposes. In what follows I would like to complicate this narrative by suggesting that the negotiation between gendered subject and object positions in the construction of heroic agency in *Tamburlaine* is considerably more complex than its normative dimensions indicate. In so doing I am not attempting to reverse, and I am not denying, the manifest intent in the play to consolidate male dominance and female submission. But I am questioning its stability by focusing more closely on the fluctuating interchange of gendered positions that constitute Tamburlaine's heroic identity. Emphasizing this dynamic not as an accomplished task, but as a fluid, never-ending process and, indeed, as a struggle, puts pressure on the systematic privileging of traditionally male terms which, in Marlowe, only partially constitute even the most unrelievedly masculine heroism.

Earlier I suggested considering the process of heroism as a gendered positioning of the self in relation to pleasure and power. When Tamburlaine and his henchmen reflect on the warrior-king's agency, the extent to which he is positioned, and positions himself, as an object is remarkable. For example, Tamburlaine objectifies Zenocrate by aestheticizing her and rendering her static. Yet, at his most awesome, Tamburlaine is himself constructed by others as an inspiring aesthetic object:

> Of stature tall, and straightly fashionèd,
> Like his desire lift upwards and divine;
> So large of limbs, his joints so strongly knit,
> Such breadth of shoulders as might mainly bear
> Old Atlas' burthen; 'twixt his manly pitch,
> A pearl, more worth than all the world, is placed,
> Wherein by curious sovereignty of art
> Are fixed his piercing instruments of sight,

Whose fiery circles bear encompassèd
A heaven of heavenly bodies in their spheres,
That guides his steps and actions to the throne,
Where honor sits invested royally.

(1.2.1.7–18)

Larger than life, the giant, pearl-headed monarch is a dehumanized figure. Conceived and appropriated by his subjects as the creative source of their own identities and power, the imagery representing Tamburlaine associates him with art, ornament, and spectacle. In short he plays a woman's part: when constructed as most magnificently male, Tamburlaine is imagined to occupy a traditionally female position.[4]

This phenomenon can be understood politically by adding gender to Christopher Pye's illuminating study of Renaissance monarchy as a created spectacle involving reflexive relations of power and desire. Pye analyzes the formation of Renaissance sovereignty as a mutually constituted process of reciprocal gazing between monarch and subjects. Accounting for this specular dynamic as part of "the irreducible relationship between theatricality and absolutism during the English Renaissance," Pye discusses the contradiction between the political subject's perception of his or her being as inhering in the sovereign's person and the simultaneous recognition of the absolute difference of the king: "[M]erely to gaze on the monarchic body, to discern it as a distinct form, was to renew the split inhabiting one's own being, and to conjure one's own origins in a divided and alien form—in spectacle."[5]

Pye argues that ultimately the contradictions between the subject's perception of himself or herself as simultaneously part of and completely different from the king were theoretically resolved to shore up absolutism (e.g., in Hobbes). But he also contends convincingly that the spectacular Renaissance monarch remains poised in tension between the sovereign's dependency upon and power over his subjects: "[T]he vulnerability and the terrifying power of the monarch's visible presence are, in fact, inseparable. . . . [T]he subject's desire to reduce the sovereign presence to the fully exposed object of his sight lends the regal eye its penetrating, and impenetrable power."[6] In turn the monarch's power would cease to exist without the subject's desiring gaze.

The description of Tamburlaine quoted above makes clear that, along with his astounding rhetorical power, the hero's strength radiates from his piercing eyes. Throughout the play his rule is represented in terms of vision and visibility: "To ask and have, command and be obeyed; / When looks breed love, with looks to gain the prize, / Such power attractive shines in princes' eyes!" (1.2.5.62–64). Inhabiting a female subject position, the spectacular monarch is completely dependent upon the subjects' collective gaze, which legitimates, indeed creates, his power. Riding in triumph through Persepolis, for example, would be impossible by definition without admiring—that is to say, subjected—onlookers. Creating and recreating himself both through language and as spectacle, Tamburlaine simultaneously acknowledges and resents this dependency, expressing an aggressive desire to seize the power of spectatorship from the onlookers upon whom he relies: "And with our sun-bright armor as we march, / We'll chase the stars from heaven and dim their eyes / That stand and muse at our admirèd arms" (1.2.3.22–24). The sovereign as spectacle keeps the subject in awe, subjected; at the same time his power depends upon his ability to command his subjects' gaze.

Seeking the solution to dependency and objectification in omnipotence, Tamburlaine attempts to monopolize all subject positions, which are, inevitably, gendered. Thus he imagines himself as watching his subjects watching him. A wonderful moment of unadulterated narcissism occurs at the end of part 2, when, dying, Tamburlaine mourns not his own departure from the world but his subjects' loss of him as their treasured, irreplaceable object of desire: "My body feels, my soul doth weep to see / Your sweet desires deprived my company, / For Tamburlaine, the scourge of God, must die" (2.5.3.247–49).

The tensions in Tamburlaine's heroism can be understood further by examining his own, often contradictory, positioning of himself in relation to the gods. First, he glibly inhabits various male positions in what is now commonly thought of as the oedipal narrative, that tale of rivalry, separation, and ultimately identification with the father, which offers an account of male identity formation.[7] Frequently Tamburlaine conflates himself with Jove in Jove's role as son, identifying with the god's parricide. For example, he describes his motivations for conquest to the defeated Cosroe as follows:

> The thirst of reign and sweetness of a crown
> That caused the eldest son of heavenly Ops,
> To thrust his doting father from his chair,
> And place himself in the empyreal heaven,
> Moved me to manage arms against thy state.
> What better precedent than mighty Jove?
> (1.2.7.12–17)

Extending this oedipal trope, Tamburlaine takes the next rhetorical step and sets himself up as Jove's rival and successor: "Zenocrate, were Egypt Jove's own land, / Yet would I with my sword make Jove to stoop" (1.4.4.78–79). Yet Tamburlaine is also gazed upon by Jove, objectified both as the god's rival—"Jove, viewing me in arms, looks pale and wan, / Fearing my power should pull him from the throne" (1.5.1.454–55)—and as his darling, the chosen object of the god's protection and admiring awe: "Jove shall send his wingèd messenger / To bid me sheathe my sword and leave the field" (2.1.3.166–67); or "Nor am I made arch-monarch of the world, / Crowned and invested by the hand of Jove / For deeds of bounty and nobility" (2.4.1.152–54).

That Tamburlaine (both character and play) never resolves the tension among his self-appointed positions in relation to the gods becomes apparent in his appropriations of the figure of Phaeton, offspring of the sun-god, Apollo, who courageously, although madly, tries but disastrously fails to drive his father's chariot over the earth. In an early identification with this figure, Tamburlaine seems unaware of the suicidal implications of the story, identifying instead with the power of its carnage:

> But ere I march to wealthy Persia,
> Or leave Damascus and the Egyptian fields,
> As was the fame of Clymene's brain-sick son,
> That almost brent the axletree of heaven,
> So shall our swords, our lances, and our shot
> Fill all the air with fiery meteors.
> (1.4.2.47–52)

Dying at the very end of the play, Tamburlaine again evokes Phaeton when exhorting his son to rule in his place (2.5.3.229–45). Timothy

Reiss makes an elegant case for the conjunction of references to Phaeton with Tamburlaine's declining heroism.[8] Yet I find that these references are sliding and ambiguous throughout both parts of the play. Tamburlaine casts himself both as Apollo and as his "brain-sick" son of a mortal mother. Is he a god or the son of a god?

Further, is he male or female; or, to put the point more precisely, does he occupy male or female subject positions? My argument is that his heroic identity requires the attempt to monopolize all subject positions. That this effort is constituent of Tamburlaine's heroism becomes readily perceptible when we consider the way he positions himself in relation to Jove in his role as seducer, lover, or friend. Despite the explicit or implicit erotic content of these passages, I do not focus on eroticism per se. My concern is to explore arbitrariness and inequality in the creation of gender difference, and my analysis explores issues of agency: positions of passivity, activity, dominance, and submission.

The most prominent of Tamburlaine's seductions—the original wooing of Zenocrate—is a rape. Whether we take "rape" to mean abduction of someone else's property in a person or forced sexual intercourse, the crucial element in both instances is compulsion.[9] It is force, then, that I am viewing as the defining characteristic of rape. Unlike Ben Jonson, whose Truewit in Epicoene defines rape as "an acceptable violence" (4.1.90), Marlowe recognizes that this method of courtship could be considered problematic; like Ben Jonson, however, he decides that women would probably have liked it, and that Zenocrate would have been pleased.[10] When confronted by one of her courtiers with "your offensive rape by Tamburlaine," Zenocrate replies that it has been "digested long ago, / As his exceeding favors have deserved, / And might content the Queen of heaven, as well / As it hath changed my first conceived disdain" (1.3.2.6; 9–12).

In any event neither Tamburlaine as conqueror nor Zenocrate as conquest presents a reversal, or any other revision, of the traditional gendered alignment of male with active subjectivity, female with passive objectivity. As a rapist, Tamburlaine once again claims Jove as both model and rival. "Amorous Jove hath snatched my love from hence," he says, describing Zenocrate's death (2.2.4.107). Yet Jupiter as rapist also appears in a less conventional form near the beginning of the play, when Tamburlaine seduces his Persian enemy Theridamas into joining forces with him. His first means of persuasion is to present himself as the successful masculine hero-subject, fully active and in charge: "I hold the fates bound fast in iron chains, / And with my hand turn fortune's wheel about" he boasts, in one of his most characteristic modes (1.1.2.176–77). But such self-presentation does not account fully for Tamburlaine's performance of his heroic identity; he must create and re-create himself not simply as an active, questing subject, but also as the chosen object of the god's love. Challenging Theridamas to wound him in order to demonstrate his invulnerability, Tamburlaine declares,

> Draw forth thy sword, thou mighty man at arms,
> Intending but to raze my charmèd skin,
> And Jove himself will stretch his hand from heaven
> To ward the blow and shield me safe from harm.
> See how he rains down heaps of gold in showers,
> As if he meant to give my soldiers pay!
>   (1.1.2.178–82)

Once we recognize the reference to showers of gold as an image of Jupiter's rape of Danae, we realize that Tamburlaine, in order most persuasively to convey the range of his powers, presents himself positively as the god's charmed darling in the figure of a raped woman. Whatever psychological, erotic, or moral valence we might choose to assign to Tamburlaine's assumption of the position of a raped woman, my point is that he clearly considers his own doing so to be a persuasive manifestation of his strength. And his persuasion works: Theridamas succumbs, proving a steadfast comrade for the duration of Tamburlaine's quest. The successful performance of omnipotence, then, is doubly gendered, in terms of both its projection and its reception. Considering the heroic as the location where textual meanings inhere, it is clear that meaningfulness in *Tamburlaine* is imagined as both male and female.

III

Marlowe begins *Dr. Faustus* (c. 1588–92) by announcing a new kind of hero, one whom he identifies negatively as neither warrior, lover, nor courtier:

> Not marching now in fields of Thrasimen
> Where Mars did mate the warlike Carthagens;
> Nor sporting in the dalliance of love,
> In courts of kings, where state is overturned;
> Nor in the pomp of proud audacious deeds,
> Intends our Muse to vaunt his heavenly verse.[11]
>
> (prologue, 1–6)

The revised performance of heroism will concentrate instead on "[t]he form of Faustus' fortunes, good or bad" (prologue, 8). One of the pressing questions in the play involves not so much the relation of the hero's desire to his agency, a question I have been exploring in *Tamburlaine,* but whether, given the nature of desire as Marlowe represents it, the hero has agency at all.

In *The Regal Phantasm: Shakespeare and the Politics of Spectacle* (cited above), Christopher Pye demonstrates that combining some of the insights of Lacanian psychoanalysis with an awareness of Renaissance historical conditions can be very useful in analyzing Renaissance texts. Lacan's account of the formation of subjectivity certainly helps to illuminate the structures of desire and agency in Marlowe, particularly in *Dr. Faustus.* According to Lacan, the subject gains a sense of identity when he or she first apprehends his or her own reflection, in what Lacan famously designates as the "mirror stage" of consciousness. Providing the subject with a sense of wholeness, the mirror image is nevertheless shrunken, inverted, and separate from the perceiving self, alien. Since desire springs from this process of perception, it is based on an inevitable misrecognition, a delusion that wholeness and coherence constitute the self. This delusion creates a necessary condition for the establishment of identity. For Lacan, the self-awareness that generates desire is paradoxically constituted by an irredeemable alienation from the self. Unable properly to recognize boundaries, the self can never truly distinguish itself from the other. Trapped, the subject experiences desire as a search, inevitably futile, for what has been lost.[12]

This specular dynamic is present in Tamburlaine, who views his enemies as the mirror of his honor (5.1.480) and sees himself as the object of others' desires. But one of the ultimate implications of Lacan's "mirror stage"—the unacknowledged (by the subject) collapse of object relations that then dooms the deluded subject—strongly informs the whole of *Dr. Faustus*. Although granted little agency, Zenocrate as object of desire in *Tamburlaine* is, at least, an embodied presence; Helen of Troy in *Dr. Faustus* is a phantom. "Mine own fantasy / . . . will receive no object," Faustus complains, before embarking on an increasingly trivialized life of narcissistic self-enclosure (1.1.105–6).

As in *Tamburlaine,* the performance of heroic identity in *Dr. Faustus* is fully articulated in the gendered positioning of the hero's self in relation to God. In *Dr. Faustus,* however, these encounters suffuse the entire play: indeed they *are* the play. The preparation for the penultimate encounter between Faustus and God occurs in the hero's seduction of the ghostly, silent Helen. Faustus begins his seduction speech by casting himself as the traditional, active male hero, the warrior-lover inspired by the beauty of the beloved to conquer his rivals in hand-to-hand combat. Although Faustus acknowledges Helen's potentially destructive erotic power ("Her lips suck forth my soul. See where it flies!" [5.1.111]), he goes on to conceptualize her in the traditional female role as inspiration of his chivalric-heroic military adventures:

> I will be Paris, and for love of thee,
> Instead of Troy, shall Wittenberg be sacked;
> And will combat with weak Menelaus,
> And wear thy colors on my plumèd crest;
> Yea, I will wound Achilles in the heel,
> And then return to Helen for a kiss.
>   (5.1.115–120)

Yet, just as Tamburlaine does in his seduction of Theridamas, Faustus switches in mid-speech from the position of initiating agent to the position of being acted upon. Specifically, he changes from identification with the male rapist (Paris) to conflation of himself with the female victim / beloved. Addressing Helen, he continues:

> Brighter art thou than flaming Jupiter
> When he appeared to hapless Semele;
> More lovely than the monarch of the sky
> In wanton Arethusa's azured arms;
> And none but thou shalt be my paramour!
>   (5.1.123–27)

Just as the gender configurations altered in *Tamburlaine*, in *Dr. Faustus* Helen becomes the god, Faustus the self-appointed female object of his / her predatory love. But Faustus's choices of mythological female figures with whom to identify make an interesting comparison with Tamburlaine's. As noted, in his seduction of Theridamas, Tamburlaine imagines himself as Danae, to whom Jupiter appears as a shower of gold, after which visitation Danae gives birth to Perseus. While it is certainly true that Danae has no say in the matter, she is not doomed: that is, she does not lose her identity.[13] Faustus, however, chooses to conflate himself with Semele, a lover of Jupiter who, although not raped, is tricked by the jealous Juno into unknowingly seeking her own extinction, a disastrous incineration. Wildly pursued, Faustus's other choice, Arethusa, escapes assault only by dissolution, hiding from her potential rapist in a cloud and eventually being metamorphosed into a fountain. "Now draw up Faustus, like a foggy mist, / Into the entrails of yon laboring cloud" (5.1.300–301), Faustus begs, hoping to conceal himself from the supernatural gaze, later adding a plea to let his soul "be changed into small water-drops, / And fall into the ocean, ne'er be found!" (5.1.326 27).

But of course there is no hiding. As one of my students put it, the demons have become part of Faustus's life. Directly following the seduction speech in the B text, the hero becomes the object of a relentless demonic gaze. "And here we'll stay, / To mark him how he doth demean himself," Belzebub announces, eagerly awaiting the spectacle of Faustus's destruction (5.1.145–46). In one sense Faustus's wish for violent extinction and dispersal—a traditionally female fate expressed in the seduction scene when he conflates himself with Semele and Arethusa—comes true. His heart is, literally, broken: "Ah, rend not my heart for naming of my Christ!" (5.1.289); and he is dismembered, discovered by his friends in the B text as a pile of mangled limbs "all torn asunder by the hand of death" (5.1.338). Watching Faustus, Mephistopheles' gloating observations point to the hero's failed masculine agency:

> Fond worldling, now his heart-blood dries with grief,
> His conscience kills it, and his laboring brain
> Begets a world of idle fantasies
> To over-reach the Devil: but all in vain.
>
> (5.1.148–51)

Faustus's final torment reveals the futility of any active endeavor on his part: "Oh, I'll leap up to my God!—Who pulls me down?" (5.1.286); or the fearful outburst, "Oh, he stays my tongue! I would lift up my hands; but see, they hold 'em, they hold 'em!" (5.1.194—96). And the hero himself sees the cause of his tragedy as rooted in the delusions and futility of his own active desires, his own seeking: "Oh, would I had never seen Wittenberg, never read book!" (5.1.182—83). The heroic subject is trapped in his own narcissism, unable to see himself seeing himself. From this perspective Faustus finds himself in the most vulnerable of all female subject positions: attempts at autonomous agency doom him to violent objectification: destruction through bodily dispersal.

Marlowe leaves the problem of active heroic agency unresolved; the capacity as well as the possibilities for active choosing remain open to question. Like Tamburlaine, Faustus is represented as a son who exists in ambivalent relation to his father. The mysterious Old Man, a benevolent father figure who enters near the end of the play and tries to save Faustus, is granted an efficacious agency, represented in soaring terms that contrast directly with Faustus's impotence: "My faith, vile hell, shall triumph over thee. / . . . / Hence, hell! for hence I fly unto my God" (5.1.133—36). On the other hand, the play's smug epilogue, which, blaming the hero for his bad choices and attempting to reassure the audience by implying that Faustus's destiny is not inevitable, presents an impossibly inadequate attempt to contain the tragic situation. The conflation of the hero with Icarus in the prologue implies that the father who creates him is also responsible for his destruction.

I am suggesting that the tragic ironies of Faustus's heroic identity become fully legible only when Marlowe's representation of an actively desiring (read male) subjectivity doomed to solipsism by its very nature is combined with his equally powerful representation of Faustus's inability to position himself adequately as an object of God's gaze, or of God's love. I have already suggested the ways in which Faustus constructs himself as the victim / object of violence; although from some perspectives, including the Renaissance equation of orgasm with death, the associations of extinction and dissolution with sexual ecstasy give these images a double edge. But the very end of the play makes clear that, for Faustus, the demonic gaze is confounded with God's. "My God, my God, look not so fierce on me!" he pleads (5.1.328); and, in an image that recalls that of Jupiter's arm in *Tamburlaine,* he adds, "[S]ee where God / Stretcheth out his arm and bends his ireful brows" (5.1.291–92). Whereas Tamburlaine basks in the admiring protection of Jove's outstretched arm, Faustus feels only anger, fear, and the need for self-concealment. Unable to imagine himself as the treasured object of God's desire, Faustus has no experience or conception of loving or being loved. "Faustus' offense can ne'er be pardoned," he says, "The serpent that tempted Eve may be saved, but not Faustus" (5.1.131–33).

IV

Faustus's conviction that he is unlovable (and so unloving) is to me a moving statement of Marlowe's own alienation. As is often observed, the Marlovian hero is a stranger, an outlaw figure, who is either deviant, socially marginal, or both.[14] Even the most successful performance of heroic identity—Tamburlaine's—does not allow the hero the privilege of surviving to build his castle within the city walls (see, e.g., 2.4.2.106–33). Among English Renaissance dramatists it is Ben Jonson whose pessimism about heroics most resembles Marlowe's. Here I refer to the Jonson of *Volpone* (1606), *Epicoene* (1609), and *The Alchemist* (1610), the period of his career when, as James Shapiro has shown, Jonson was most under the influence of Marlowe.[15]

While both writers have distinct contempt for the human species, Marlowe is detached, alienated beyond rage or even misanthropy. In contrast, Jonson in his darker moods hates people, but he hates them, as it were, with a passion: his is an engaged contempt. In Jonson's plots anger, disgust, and deceit invariably are contained, no matter how grudgingly, in deference to the necessity of community, a process that makes Jonson a comic writer. Yet scholars have been pointing for years to the overdetermination of Jonson's comic actions, particularly with reference to the punishing end of *Volpone*.[16] Before turning to *Macbeth,* I would like briefly to examine Volpone's performance of his identity when, in the quest for pleasure and power, he positions and repositions himself in gendered terms.

Just as Marlowe does in *Dr. Faustus,* Jonson begins *Volpone* by defining the hero's agency negatively—defining him, that is, by what he doesn't do:

> I use no trade, no venture;
> I wound no earth with ploughshares, fat no beasts
> To feed the shambles; have no mills for iron,
> Oil, corn, or men, to grind 'hem into powder;
> I blow no subtle glass, expose no ships
> To threat'nings of the furrow-facèd sea;
> I turn no monies in the public bank,
> Nor usury private.[17]
>
>   (1.1.33–40)

Volpone's nonproductive inactivity extends to the family, of which he has none. And it is precisely this lack of creative effort or attachment that makes him both the manipulating subject and the self-appointed object of the gaze: "I have no wife, no parent, child, ally, / To give my substance to: but whom I make / Must be my heir; and this makes men observe me"(1.1.73–75). To watch himself watching others watching him—in other words, to occupy all subject positions at once, thus annihilating all objects—is Volpone's goal.

Just as Marlowe represents heroic desire tragically in Dr. Faustus, so Jonson in Volpone constructs it comically as a solipsistic process with no purposefulness, no particular consequences beyond the elaboration of self-love. Volpone consciously celebrates the self-perpetuating endlessness of desire by stressing the insignificance of the object sought: "I glory / More in the cunning purchase of my wealth / Than in the glad possession, since I gain / No common way," he gloats (1.1.30–33); and he later adds that the pleasure of outwitting others is superior to the pleasures of sex (5.1.27–28).

That Volpone's phallic heroism seeks to monopolize all gendered subject positions—to exist simultaneously as both subject and object of the gaze—becomes readily apparent when he attempts to seduce Celia (3.3.144–240). His eloquence in this instance involves presenting and re-presenting himself and Celia as spectators, their theatricalized love as spectacle, the form in which they can enact—and admire themselves while enacting—Ovidian tales of love and rape. Volpone's heroic identity encompasses multiple levels of the idea of performance, since he applies all of his energies toward the creation of roles, thus literalizing the metaphor of identity as theater.

Volpone's active, energetic wit and his manipulative, absurdly brave assumption of control—including his attempt to annihilate all objects of desire by assimilating them into his own identity—are tendencies that place his performance squarely within the domain of traditional male heroics. Yet it is remarkable the extent to which, precisely in order to perform this male identity, Volpone is placed, and places himself, in female subject positions. Eagerly assenting to his patron's self-celebratory refusal to assume an occupation (quoted above), Mosca points to a distinctly nonphallic dimension of Volpone's agency: "You are not like the thresher that doth stand / With a huge flail, watching a heap of corn," Mosca rejoices (1.1.53–54). Significantly, Volpone's attempt to rape Celia is a disaster. Like Faustus's leap up to God, Volpone's leap off the sickbed fails. The theme of his failed masculinity eventually issues in his disguise of impotence.

More important than Volpone's inadequate erotic performance is the fact that the major role he chooses to play—his part in relation to the legacy-hunting gulls—is distinctly female. Languishing on his couch, passive, immobilized, silenced, body parts gazed upon, dissected, and fragmented, courted and wooed by predatory suitors whose hopes he teases, frustrates, and rekindles: Volpone becomes a grotesque parody of the beloved mistress in a Petrarchan sonnet.[18] The hero's lyrical career as a sonnet lady is clarified by a direct inversion of traditionally gendered positions when an aggressive verbal assault by the dreaded Lady Wouldbe reduces him to silence. After hinting to her that "your highest female grace is silence" (3.2.109), Volpone quickly realizes that he is in no position to command; in order to cut short the encounter, he himself must "profess obstinate silence; / That's now my safest" (3.2.117–18). Appropriating the male prerogative of speech, Lady Wouldbe discourses about literature, contemplating without end the differences among Petrarch, Guarini, and Montaigne: "Your Petrarch is more passionate," she reflects, "yet he, / In days of sonnetting, trusted 'hem with much" (3.2.124–25).

There is a dark underside to Volpone's occupation of female subject positions, which emerges most clearly in the form of violence against women, specifically violence against Celia. Celia is not only made the target of rape; her jealous husband, the gull Corvino, also drags her by the hair and threatens her with a terrifying array of physical abuses. Corvino's threats to Celia make clear that Jonson is Marlowe's equal in the representation of violence[19]:

> Be damned!
> Heart, I will drag thee hence home by the hair;
> Cry thee a strumpet through the streets; rip up
> Thy mouth unto thine ears; and slit thy nose,
> Like a raw rochet! . . .
> I will buy some slave
> Whom I will kill, and bind thee to him alive!
> And at my window hang you forth, devising
> Some monstrous crime, which I, in capital letters,
> Will eat into thy flesh with *aquafortis*
> And burning corsives, on this stubborn breast.
>   (3.3.99–109)

Not surprisingly, Celia's only recourse is that of the victim: to meet violent assault with self-abuse. In the rape scene she tells Volpone,

> [I will] flay my face,
> Or poison it with ointment for seducing
> Your blood to this rebellion. Rub these hands
> With what may cause an eating leprosy,
> E'en to my bones and marrow.
> . . . .
> And I will kneel to you, pray for you, pay down
> A thousand hourly vows, sir, for your health.
>   (3.3.255–62)

The hero's trajectory as a courted lady in fact imitates Celia's, particularly in its masochism. The similarity between hero and victim becomes clear in a scene with Volpone, Mosca, and Corvino. Pretending that the silent, passive, prostrate Volpone is deaf, Mosca seizes the opportunity to shriek abuse into his ear. "Those filthy eyes of yours, that flow with slime, / Like two frog-pits; and those same hanging cheeks,

/ Covered with hide instead of skin," he screams with glee; and Corvino enthusiastically joins in: "His nose is like a common sewer, still running." The two happily continue their duet until the sadistic impulse behind it is nakedly revealed, specifically in terms of female aggression: "Faith I could stifle him rarely with a pillow / As well as any woman that should keep him," Mosca confides; to which Corvino responds, "Do as you will; but I'll begone," adding, "I pray you use no violence" (1.1.519–21, 527, 530–32, 534). That Volpone's eventual response to this scene is rapturously to commend Mosca can suffice to make the audience aware of the aggressive perversity of the hero's plot to outwit his foes. For what he actually does is dramatize to himself how little he is cared for, how everyone hates him and wishes he were dead. "They never think of me," he later acknowledges, in an uncharacteristically forlorn moment of self-reflection (5.1.146).

V

"My way of life / Is fall'n into the sere, the yellow leaf, / And that which should accompany old age, / As honour, love, obedience, troops of friends, / I must not look to have," Macbeth reflects matter-of-factly (5.3.23–27).[20] Like Faustus and Volpone, Macbeth toward the end of his heroic career recognizes his alienation; unlike Faustus or Volpone, however, he feels neither self-pity nor fear. "Hang those that talk of fear," he instructs, and means it (5.3.38). Further unlike his counterparts, Macbeth meets his fate without ambivalence: "I have lived long enough," he acknowledges (5.3.23). That his courage and certainty are tantamount to despair does not negate his eerie integrity, the fact that he accepts full responsibility for his actions; it makes that acceptance more astonishing and terrifying. Overcoming insomnia and hallucinations, he resolves to "tell pale-hearted fear it lies, / And sleep in spite of thunder" (4.1.101–2). Knowing that he is about to be defeated and feeling no compelling reason to live, his response is that of the consummate soldier: "I'll fight till from my bones my flesh be hacked. / Give me my armour. . . . / . . . / At least we'll die with harness on our back" (5.3.33–34; 5.5.50).

Composed during a five-year period (1603–8) and excluding only *King Lear,* four out of five of Shakespeare's late tragedies (*Othello*

[1603–4], *Macbeth* and *Antony and Cleopatra* [1606], and *Coriolanus* [1608]) focus insistently on the unequaled feats of an individual male warrior. Whether it is represented romantically as exotic or construed fiercely as alienated, whether it is constructed elegiacally as anachronistic or mourned as nostalgic, aristocratic male militarism, replete with grandeur and failure, becomes the vehicle that carries tragic meaning. As I have analyzed at length elsewhere, Othello's legendary military excellence seems to exist in direct proportion to his marital tragedy. His contempt for domestic detail, need to act rapidly, physical fearlessness, lack of reflective acknowledgment of his own emotional vulnerabilities, and abstract sense of justice become the components used to dramatize his failure to grasp the heroic significance of private life.[21]

Like Othello, Mark Antony fails to integrate his public and private lives, a fact that generates his tragedy. Throughout *Antony and Cleopatra* Antony's military heroism is frequently lamented by both friends (Enobarbus, 4.6.30–39; 4.10.11–22) and enemies (Caesar, 1.4.55–71) as a thing of the past. Alternately scathing or mournful in tone, the play's internal critique of Antony often takes gendered form. He is mistaken for Cleopatra, dresses in her clothes, takes her military advice against his better judgment, and incurs disastrous defeat by fleeing a battle, both in pursuit and in imitation of her. Charismatic and unsteady, Antony is also hopelessly ambivalent, unable to commit himself either to Rome or to Egypt. While his rejection of Roman militarism is neither complete nor decisive, however, it is self-conscious and, as such, clearly part of his greatness. The traditional triumph of conquest belongs to the remote and boyish Caesar, who shrewdly refuses Antony's offer to undertake personal combat between them: apparently Antony's brand of heroic masculinity, if bold and loyal, is nevertheless unwise and out of style. But Caesar's mean-spirited and limited experience of life, no matter how powerfully self-preserving, is diminished in comparison to that of Antony or Cleopatra. Like most tragic figures, Antony is unfit for the present; exceeding the capacities of the historical moment in which he lives, his greatness is rapidly receding into the past. His divided heroism, however, gestures beyond tragedy into the future. Not only does he share the stage with a powerful woman, she outlives him and has the last word, which she uses to eulogize, characterize, and, it could be argued, mystify him: it is as though Hamlet's and Othello's wishes to be favorably remembered in the future were summoned imaginatively into the present, embodied and enacted on stage.

After his damaging, eventually fatal defeat at Actium, Antony comforts his followers: "Know my hearts, / I hope well of tomorrow, and will lead you / Where rather I'll expect victorious life / Than death and honour" (4.2.41–44). As his bungled attempt to kill himself indicates, Antony lacks the isolating suicidal impulse of other tragic heroes. That rush toward self-sacrifice, present in varying degrees in all warrior heroes, is at its most prominent in *Coriolanus*. Interestingly, whereas Antony's full identity is not limited to traditional masculinity (i.e., his status as a warrior), Coriolanus, whose identity is completely invested in aristocratic militarism, is not fully a man. The play repeatedly makes clear that he is, as his enemy Aufidius describes him, a "boy of tears" (5.6.103). Janet Adelman has analyzed the hero's stunted growth as directly related to the monstrous nurturance of his mother, who values nothing but Roman military victory and its accompanying violence, whether or not that violence will destroy her son.[22] "There's no man in the world / More bound to's mother" (5.3.159–60), Volumnia boasts; but the Tribunes speculate ominously: "They say she's mad" (4.2.11).

Coriolanus experiences very little love; like Othello, he feels love only to be destroyed as a result. While Othello fails to acknowledge the importance of the personal dimensions of his life, however, the life of Coriolanus lacks those dimensions almost completely. Like Tamburlaine without that hero's charisma or charm, Coriolanus becomes a killing machine. His emotional range is limited primarily to hostility and contempt. When he is banished from Rome, he can think of no place better to go than to the home of his worst enemy. He seems to have no choice: either he must inflict death or seek and embrace it. Thus *Coriolanus* isolates with an insistent, almost glaring focus the bleak element of antisocial self-destructiveness inherent in active male heroism.

Coriolanus is Shakespeare's last tragedy, and the scrutiny of heroic masculinity it presents is penetrating but one-dimensional; the critique is almost exhausted. In contrast, the earlier figure, Macbeth, is set apart from other Shakespearean warriors of noble stature by the way in which his heroic idealism grows almost to perfection, increasing in severity and intensity throughout the play. More than any other figure, he embodies with alarming purity the Renaissance ideal of the active male hero in its most complete and pristine form, exposing its logic. Paradoxically, precisely because of its unique purity, Macbeth's achievement of undiluted masculinism illuminates with perfect and rigorous clarity the shared values and beliefs that the culture uses to construct heroism.

When I was in college and graduate school, considerations of *Macbeth* tended to focus on the motivations for the hero's evil in distinctly gendered terms: is it her ambition or his that is the cause of the terror? does Lady Macbeth corrupt her husband from "the milk of human kindness" to a bloody and tyrannical career? or does Macbeth's susceptibility to his first encounter with the witches manifest his already overly ambitious nature, on which his wife feeds? Actually the play yields very little information in response to these questions. The psychological exploration of motive and the moral inquiry into "ambition" receive only truncated treatment. I think that is because *Macbeth* is not about ambition, it is about murder—not murder that occurs before the action, as in *Hamlet*; nor killings and deaths that fill the stage in the final scene, as in *Hamlet, Othello,* and *King Lear*; instead in Macbeth murder *is* the action, escalating with dire and drastic rapidity throughout the play.

What does it mean for the hero of a play to embrace murder as what he calls "my way of life"? Tamburlaine's public, arrogant slaughters, conducted impersonally and with open pride in the name of glorious conquest, command loyalty and devotion from his followers. In contrast, Macbeth's murders are secret and treacherous, perpetrated against his own subjects, so that the detested tyrant can keep himself in power. As Adelman has brilliantly shown, Macbeth's heroic performance involves finding a kind of final solution to the problem of gender difference.[23] Unlike Tamburlaine, Volpone, and Faustus, who appropriate the advantages of female subjectivity in order to achieve their heroic identities, Macbeth achieves his by seeking to eliminate any association whatsoever with the female, to escape entirely the condition of being "born of woman." Unlike any other hero, Macbeth succeeds in this mission to a remarkable extent. In a grotesque parody of the chivalric female function of inspiring the warrior-hero, Lady Macbeth and the witches permeate the play with a malignity that both demands responsive action and requires desperate escape from those demands. "Art thou afeard / To be the same in thine own act and valour / As thou art in desire?" Lady Macbeth taunts her husband at the beginning of the play (1.7.39–41); and echoing her waking self later in her most famous scene, adds, "A soldier and afeard?" (5.1.31–32). By the end Macbeth has murdered not only sleep, but fear. Recalling a lost past when fright could make his hair stand on end, he resolves after Macduff's flight, "From this moment / The very firstlings of my heart shall be / The firstlings of my hand" (4.1.162–64). He has already rejected the intimacy of his marriage, ceasing to confide in and conspire with his wife. Simultaneously and in contrast, Lady Macbeth surrenders to sleep, fear, and guilt and even to a little pity. She disappears from the action and, after one additional outburst in the sleepwalking scene, dies, at a time when mourning is no longer an option for those who survive.

One approach to understanding the interrogation of heroic idealism in *Macbeth* is to examine the similarities between the positions of Macbeth and Macduff, the enemy-savior who finally destroys the hero-tyrant. Explored in moral terms, this relationship reveals Macbeth as the bloody aggressor whose unmatched cruelty perpetrates the murder of Macduff's entire family while the latter is away trying to save Scotland. Whatever his faults, Macduff is the wronged party, the victim of this unspeakable union of personal and political crimes. Whether or not it is accurate, the moral perspective has distinct limitations. Macduff's family is vulnerable because he has abandoned them, a fact to which the play calls repeated attention. "Was my father a traitor, mother?" asks Macduff's little son, right before the murderers enter to destroy him; "Ay, that he was," Lady Macduff replies (4.2.44–45). As if the direct staging of the murders of Macduff's innocent and appealing family were not enough, Malcolm also confronts Macduff about leaving them unprotected, asking, "Why in that rawness left you wife and child, / Those precious motives, those strong knots of love, / Without leavetaking?" Like Tamburlaine subduing thoughts of Zenocrate, Macduff replies abstractly to a cruel situation that demands a concrete response. "Bleed, bleed, poor country!" (4.3.27–29, 32), he laments inappropriately, ignoring the insistently individualized demands of love.

It soon becomes clear if it were not already what priority this culture gives to love. When the murders of his family are announced and Macduff expresses shock and grief, Malcolm urges him to stop lamenting and "dispute it like a man." "I shall do so," Macduff responds, "[b]ut I must also feel it as a man" (4.3.221–23). Here Macduff directly echoes Macbeth's earlier reply to his wife's taunts of cowardice, made when he hesitates about killing the king: "I dare do all that may become a man; / Who dares do more is none" (1.7.46–47). Each soldier's challenge to the dominant cultural view of masculinity is of course feeble and without duration. Macbeth never repeats his claim to moral feeling; Macduff transforms his sorrow to revenge in the course of only a few lines. "This tune goes manly," Malcolm responds (4.3.237); Macduff's ability instantly to convert sorrow into homicidal rage is what finally convinces Malcolm of Macduff's loyalty.

One more analogy between the soldiers with similar-sounding names will help to make my final point. In the beginning of the play, we hear of Macbeth before we see him. After a mention of Macbeth by the witches in the first scene, we hear in the second a wounded soldier's admiring, awestruck account of Macbeth's valiance in hand-to-hand combat, the defining posture of the warrior-hero:

> For brave Macbeth—well he deserves that name!—
> Disdaining fortune, with his brandished steel
> Which smoked with bloody execution,
> Like valour's minion
> Carved out his passage till he faced the slave,
> Which ne'er shook hands nor bade farewell to him
> Till he unseamed him from the nave to th'chops,
> And fixed his head upon our battlements.
>   (1.2.16–23)

This picture predicts with accurate irony Macbeth's own fate. When in the final scene Macduff appears waving Macbeth's decapitated head, the play has come full circle. This ghastly moment is immediately preceded by the older Siward's expressions of pleasure and relief that his son has been killed paying "a soldier's debt" (5.11.5). What is ambivalently imagined in Marlowe—that fathers destroy their sons—is imagined clearly in *Macbeth,* where one faction of killers replaces another. To paraphrase from elsewhere, this *is* the promised end.

Whether the form the heroic takes is called power, magnificence, conquest, exploration, rule, discovery, or glorious war, Shakespeare in *Macbeth* clarifies that at the heart of active male heroism is not only action, but violent action; not only violent action, but death; and not only death, but violent death of a particular kind: murder. In one of his final investigations of aristocratic male heroism, Shakespeare interprets its extreme logic as tragic, but also as criminal. Interestingly, because it is so thorough and devastating, the critique of masculinity embedded in *Macbeth* destroys the heroic ideal while at the same time mourning its destruction in the play's moving portrait of the hero's courage. Nevertheless, the annihilating totality of the play's exposure of male heroism as criminal violence gestures toward the future trajectory of the heroic. As the seventeenth century progresses, the terms in which heroism is constructed come increasingly to resemble the terms in which women are idealized; the heroic, in other words, becomes increasingly female.

In the historical period I analyze, the primary female hero, Elizabeth I, emerges at the beginning of this process, creating her heroic identity in the mid- to late sixteenth century. As in Marlowe and Jonson and in certain cases Shakespeare, the terms in which Elizabeth establishes her heroism are multiply gendered, articulating a drive toward omnipotence best described as the attempt to monopolize all gendered subject positions. As I will show, Elizabeth undertakes this quest knowingly and openly; and, unlike other Renaissance heroes with similar goals, she survives.

TWO

Gender and the Construction of Royal Authority in the Speeches of Elizabeth I

What manner of person was this—nay more, what quality of
woman in so masculine a society—that dared stand in the isola-
tion of her own instinct and authority against her whole world?
J. E. Neale, *Elizabeth I and Her Parliaments: 1559–1581*

I

The most comprehensive modern authority to date on Elizabeth Tudor, J. E. Neale, presents the subject of his study in heroic terms,
emphasizing her conflicts, her courage, her commitment, and her isola-
tion.[1] Interestingly, Neale locates Elizabeth's heroism in her successful
struggle to reconcile her gender with her authority, and he ultimately
brings this issue to bear on the unique personality of the queen. While
Neale's focus on Elizabeth's personal mystery is romantic, his conception has not been effectively superseded by more skeptical generations.
Despite repeated revisionary attempts by various historians since
Neale, who have detailed at length Elizabeth's frequent duplicity, parsi-
mony, vanity, egotism, indecision, petty cruelty, and lack of sympathy
for innovation, no one has ever entirely succeeded in demystifying her.[2]
Considered from any angle, Elizabeth Tudor does indeed have a perpetually astonishing career.

Like Neale, I locate Elizabeth's heroic identity in the ways she constructs her political authority in gendered terms. Insofar as he considers
gender, Neale concludes that Elizabeth's political achievement constitutes an awe-inspiring victory over the odds. Neale *concludes* precisely
where I begin. I am not seeking to demystify Elizabeth's feats, which,
like Neale, I see as extraordinary. Instead of admiring the queen's

strength as somehow magical or inexplicable though, I want to begin to explain it and, particularly, to analyze certain of the queen's gendered self-definitions that, I argue, point to the core of her achievement. Rather than focusing on her personality or behavior per se, I am concerned with the way Elizabeth, as the central figure in and of the English nation, uses her verbal powers to define her authority and legitimize her actions in gendered terms.

Elizabeth's speeches are the texts in which, as a genre, these changing political self-representations unfold. As the recent edition of her collected works makes clear, she was a prolific writer throughout her life. From childhood through old age she continually produced poems, prayers, translations, voluminous letters, and after her coronation in 1558, eloquent, forceful speeches.[3] In her public speeches the queen justifies her political decisions (and non-decisions), repeatedly seeking to establish the terms of her legitimacy as the reigning monarch. It is in the speeches, therefore, that she cogently formulates her heroic identity, which I am equating with her conception of her royal authority.

My analysis of Elizabeth's public speeches will show that (like Dr. Faustus and Volpone) she creates her heroic persona by monopolizing all gendered positions, taking rhetorical advantage of the special prestige of both female and male subject positions as these were understood in the Renaissance without consistently privileging either. I will demonstrate that her representation of her authority changes throughout her reign, expanding from an exclusive insistence on the hierarchical privileges of a monarch to a more flexible conception that includes reliance on hierarchy but also develops a notion of rule that involves a crucial, indeed a defining, reciprocity between her subjects and herself. Further, I will show that these changes occur as marriage ceases to be a contested issue between the queen and her subjects.

II

Elizabeth I's speeches are excerpted and quoted often. Historians have analyzed them as policy statements, evidence charting the queen's relations with Parliament and the development of Parliament as an institution. Certain addresses deemed to be of particular interest, like the Golden Speech (1601), have been reproduced often by historians since the Renaissance, although usually as isolated texts meant to illustrate a point. In addition, there has been a considerable amount of recent work on the texts of individual speeches. While all of the speeches are forceful and interesting, some have passages of widely acknowledged elegance, and literary scholars have used them, usually in conjunction with works of fiction, in attempts to determine the ways Elizabethan subjects received and accommodated their powerful queen.[4]

Recently Leah Marcus has altered our view of the canon of Elizabeth's speeches by demonstrating that often the queen wrote them out in one form, spontaneously altered her text as she spoke it, then released it for publication in yet a third form. The scholarship of both Marcus and Janel Mueller clarifies that different versions of speeches were produced for different purposes; the precise historical context of each is an important part of its meaning. Consequently, instead of conflating the texts of different versions of speeches as in previous scholarship, the recent *Collected Works* includes multiple versions of speeches where these exist, leaving out only those that vary by at most a few words from those reproduced in the edition.[5] As a result, it is possible to study Elizabeth's speeches either as one genre among others in which she wrote or as a growing and evolving body of work with issues, rhetorical strategies, and self-representations that change considerably over the forty-five years of her reign. No matter what occasion prompts the speeches—the question of the queen's marrying and of the succession; the execution of Mary Stuart, Queen of Scots; the invasion of the Spanish Armada—they are all concerned with establishing Elizabeth's royal authority, and with establishing it very precisely in gendered terms.

Two distinctive but related and overlapping bodies of research have focused on Elizabeth's uses of imagery and metaphor to represent her gender to political advantage. Frances Yates, Roy Strong, and more recently, Philippa Berry examine what Strong influentially terms the "cult of Elizabeth," which associates the queen with such mythological and religious figures as Deborah, Diana, and, by implication, the Virgin Mary and valorizes her virginity in paintings, fiction, progresses, and theatrical entertainments. Not surprisingly, the cult's mystified emphasis on the magical properties of the queen's virginity flourishes at the end of her reign, when her biological age prohibits the perpetuation of the Tudor dynasty through the procreation of the monarch. Literary scholars also have identified Neoplatonism and Petrarchism as two discursive systems which, when inscribing the Elizabethan monarchy, conspire to idealize the Virgin Queen by highlighting her powerful position as the ultimate, unattainable object of desire.

In contrast, other literary / historical work embeds Elizabeth both in systems of imagery and in actual time and historical experience, analyzing the complex network of power relations that comprises Elizabethan culture. This research tends to consider Elizabeth I as a cultural phenomenon, jointly exploring selections from her writings, commentary about the queen and the events of her reign, and contemporaries' reactions to her, expressed in both fictional and nonfictional texts. Investigating the representational systems that create, describe, and express Elizabeth, the goal, as Louis Montrose eloquently states it, is to illuminate "a process of *subjectification* that, on the one hand, shapes individuals as loci of consciousness and initiators of action; and, on the other hand, positions, motivates, and constrains them within networks of power beyond their comprehension or control."[6]

Although Montrose argues cogently for an interdependent, dialectical relation between individual agent and collective structures, he concludes that ultimately Elizabeth "was more the creature of the Elizabethan image than she was its creator. Her power to shape her own strategies was itself shaped—at once enabled and constrained—by the existing repertoire of values, institutions, and practices (including the artistic and literary conventions) specific to Elizabethan society and to Elizabeth's position within it."[7] More recently, Susan Frye disagrees. "Although Elizabeth was fashioned by her culture's complex expressions of gender roles and distinctions," Frye contends, "those expressions were unstable enough to be inverted, extended, and contested in the public performance of herself as the ruler of England."[8]

Thanks to Montrose's comprehensive theoretical formulations, my analysis can focus on Elizabeth's gendered representations of her authority in her speeches not by arguing for intentionality, but by viewing the speeches as participating in an ongoing cultural dialogue. Like Frye,

I believe that the queen understands and exploits the fact that gender roles and distinctions in Elizabethan England are more malleable and unstable than has been suggested previously. It remains, however, to demonstrate precisely the nature and range of the Elizabethan performance of gender. My analysis of Elizabeth's speeches will show how she both opposes and draws on traditional female and traditional male rhetorics of authority when creating her heroic persona.

III

Existing scholarship has demonstrated the seemingly (but not actually) obvious fact that Elizabeth's gender was a problem. It is well known to what fatal lengths Henry VIII went to make sure he had a son as his legal heir. But the king's monumental endeavors to secure a male line of succession for the Tudor dynasty are now the object of historical irony, for his wishes, of course, did not in any long-range sense come true. His one legitimate son, Edward, died as a mere boy after only a few years on the throne, and the rest of the century after his death belonged to queens.

Henry's aversion to female rule was far from singular. It was shared by most of Renaissance culture, which preserved a hierarchy explicitly assuming that the subordination of women to men was a natural, indeed a supernatural, fact, and systematically excluding women from the public domain.[9] The controversy aroused by the subject of female rule extended from the accession of Mary Tudor (1553) to Elizabeth's death (1603). Unlike France, England had no law prohibiting a female monarch; yet the English debate about female rule centers on the issue of legitimacy. The most censorious, notorious negative contribution comes from the Scottish reformer John Knox, a Protestant extremist and opponent of the Catholic Mary I. Knox's *First Blast of the Trumpet against the Monstrous Regiment of Women* appeared in 1558, the year of Elizabeth's accession. "To promote a woman to bear rule, superiority, dominion, or empire above any realm, nation, or city, is repugnant to Nature. . . . [I]t is the subversion of good order, of all equity and justice," Knox contends.[10] Others (e.g., Calvin and Spenser) believe that women in general are not equipped to exercise political authority, but claim that God sometimes sees fit to endow certain exceptional women rulers with the necessary qualifications. Even supporters, however, find themselves unable to avoid the contradictions that female monarchy inevitably presents to Elizabethan social structures. John Aylmer, an opponent of Knox, expresses these problems in terms of the Queen's potential marriage: "Say you, God hath appointed her to be subject to her husband . . . therefore she may not be the head. I grant that, so far as pertaining to the bands of marriage, and the offices of a wife, she must be a subject: but as a Magistrate she may be her husband's head. . . . Why may not the woman be the husband's inferior in matters of wedlock, and his head in the guiding of the commonwealth." While trying to mitigate Elizabeth's anomalous status, Aylmer's words in fact underscore it.[11]

At the beginning of Elizabeth's reign, her encounters with Parliament clarify a lack of faith in the possibility of a single female monarch's success; this pessimism takes concrete form in Parliament's attempts to persuade her to marry, accompanied by the implicit hope that she would share power with a male consort. Terrified at the prospect of civil war should the queen fail to marry and produce an heir, Parliament continually urges her to name her successor. The struggle in which Parliament attempts alternately to plead, persuade, and coerce the queen to marry, designate an heir, or both continues for approximately the first twenty years of her forty-five-year reign. As is demonstrated by the fact that the obsession with the queen's sexuality and gender continues in one form or another throughout her reign, Elizabeth I finds herself in a political battleground, even (perhaps especially) when occupying the throne with relative security.

Emphasizing the ways that being a woman constrained and paradoxically enabled Elizabeth, existing studies of the queen offer two primary arguments about her methods of dealing with the problematics of her gender. First, it is widely contended that Elizabeth identifies herself strongly and frequently with the traditional female roles of virgin and mother. As noted, the work of Yates and Strong, and more recently Philippa Berry and Helen Hackett, emphasizes the implicit associations of Elizabeth's iconography with the Virgin Mary. "Throughout her reign, in a metaphor her sex made plausible," argues Allison Heisch, "she pictures and presents herself as a loving and yet virginal mother."

Referring to one of the queen's early speeches, Montrose observes confidently that "Elizabeth perpetuates her maidenhood in a cult of virginity; transfers her wifely duties from the household to the state; and invests her maternity in her political rather than in her natural body." Frye adds that "her metaphoric motherhood was eventually turned more to her advantage by recasting her subjects as her dependents" and contends that Elizabeth cultivates her virginity throughout her reign.[12]

Attributing such emphases to the queen's own strategic thinking, these sweeping arguments are assumed rather than demonstrated. From the evidence of the speeches, they are wrong. It is true that Elizabeth frames, as it were, the body of her speeches with self-legitimizing references to her virginity. In an early (1559), widely quoted rejoinder to Parliament's demands that she marry and name a successor, she famously remarks, "[I]n the end this shall be for me sufficient: that a marble stone shall declare that a queen, having reigned such a time, lived and died a virgin" (58). And in her final speech (1601), she reminds her subjects, "I have diminished my own revenue that I might add to your security, and been content to be a taper of true virgin wax, to waste myself and spend my life that I might give light and comfort to those that live under me" (347). Elizabeth's only other marked reference to her virginity occurs in her second speech on the execution of Mary, Queen of Scots (1586), when she attempts to establish her own innocence by lamenting, "What will they not now say when it shall be spread that for the safety of her life, a maiden queen could be content to spill the blood even of her own kinswoman?" (201).

Regarding motherhood, she tells her subjects in one version of the 1559 speech that "as many as are English, are my children" (59). Petitioning the queen to marry in 1563, Parliament refers twice to her "most gracious and motherly care" (73) and her "most honorable and motherly carefulness" (76). In response Elizabeth darkly warns, "I trust you likewise do not forget that by me you were delivered whilst you were hanging on the bough ready to fall into the mud—yea, to be drowned in the dung," adding in a softer conclusion, "And so I assure you all that though after my death you may have many stepdames, yet shall you never have any a more mother than I mean to be unto you all" (72). Other than some veiled allusions, after 1563 direct references to the queen's motherhood disappear from her speeches, even when, as she does frequently, she presents herself as nurturer and caretaker.[13]

Not only does Elizabeth fail to develop the explicit references to her virginity and motherhood that occur in her early speeches on marriage and the succession, she also qualifies or denies these allusions even in the speeches in which they are adduced. On the one hand she refers to her virginity positively, if vaguely, as a preference, stating, "I may say unto you that from my years of understanding, sith I first had consideration of myself to be born a servitor of almighty God, I happily chose this kind of life in which I yet live" (56). Far from committing herself to virginity, however, she declares her intention to renounce it. Replying to a Parliamentary petition in 1563, she protests vehemently, "I had thought it had been so desired as none other tree's blossoms should have been minded or ever hoped if my fruit had been denied you. And yet, by the way of one due doubt—that I am, as it were, by vow or determination bent never to trade that kind of life—pull out that heresy, for your belief there is awry. For though I can think it best for a private woman, yet do I strive with myself to think it not meet for a prince. And if I can bend my liking to your need I will not resist such a mind" (79). "I did send them answer by my Council I would marry, although of mine own disposition I was not inclined thereunto . . . and therefore I say again I will marry as soon as I can conveniently," she lies in 1566, continuing irritably, "And I hope to have children; otherwise I would never marry" (95). Her early (1559) declaration that "every one of you, and as many as are English, are my children" (59) precedes her second direct reference to maternity in the same speech, expressing fear that her own biological motherhood could produce unnatural children: "For although I be never so careful of your well-doings, and mind ever so to be, yet may my issue grow out of kind and become, perhaps, ungracious" (58).

Given the realities of English Renaissance constructions of gender and sexuality, that Elizabeth refrains in her public rhetoric from identifying fervently and consistently with the roles of virgin and mother is unsurprising; indeed it makes sense. Since the Reformation in the 1530s, Protestantism, newly and vehemently idealizing marriage, had gone about opposing celibacy as unnatural and so inferior to faithful married love. Thus in an unusual allusion to the moral superiority of her virginity—"If I were a milkmaid with a pail on mine arm, whereby my private person might be little set by, I would not forsake that single state to match myself with the greatest monarch. Not that I condemn the double knot or judge amiss of such as, forced by necessity, cannot dispose themselves to another life, but wish that none were driven to change save such as cannot keep honest limits"—Elizabeth relies on a respect for the prestige of celibacy that, however it echoes St. Paul, is nevertheless anachronistic (170). Not surprisingly, such allusions are rare, and, although inserted in the dialogue, not insisted upon. Nor did motherhood provide a comfortable or comforting role in which the queen could cast herself. As I have argued at length elsewhere, although there were various constructions of motherhood in Renaissance England, and although these were changing, all ideological agendas about the family agreed more or less ambivalently that maternity was incompatible with the public domain. The direct evocation of the queen as mother was far more likely to stimulate anxiety than to provide reassurance.[14] After her early speeches on marriage and the succession, then, Elizabeth virtually gives up on emphasizing the trope of virgin mother as a salient aspect of her self-presentation.

The second major argument about Elizabeth's reiterated self-inscription as the legitimate successor in a divinely sanctioned, symbolically male dynasty, while it is much more accurate, is nevertheless incomplete. Scholars have demonstrated that in the contested capacity of female ruler, Elizabeth functions politically by disarmingly acknowledging her femininity and then erasing it through appropriating the prestige of male kingship.[15] Early in the reign (1563), when addressing Parliament on the subject of her marriage, for example, she observes that "the weight and greatness of this matter might cause in me, being a woman wanting both wit and memory, some fear to speak and bashfulness besides, a thing appropriate to my sex. But yet the princely seat and kingly throne wherein God (though unworthy) hath constituted me, maketh these two causes to seem little in mine eyes, though grievous perhaps to your ears" (70). With more anger as well as more confidence, in 1566 she employs this technique by comparing herself to her father: "As for my own part, I care not for death, for all men are mortal; and though I be a woman, yet I have as good a courage answerable to my place as ever my father had" (97). Still more famously, in 1588 she exhorts the troops assembled on the field at Tilbury, waiting to engage the Spanish Armada: "I know I have the body but of a weak and feeble woman, but I have the heart and stomach of a king and of a king of England too" (326). One final example comes from the justly loved Golden Speech of 1601: "And though you have had and may have many princes more mighty and wise sitting in this seat, yet you never had or shall have any that will be more careful and loving. Shall I ascribe anything to myself and my sexly weakness? I were not worthy to live then, and of all most unworthy of the mercies I have had from God, who hath ever yet given me a heart which yet never feared any foreign or home enemy" (340). In statements like these, it is correctly argued, Elizabeth creates herself as sui generis, an exceptional woman whose royal status and unique capabilities make her inimitable. Her rhetorical technique involves appeasing widespread fears about female rule by adhering to conventions that assume the inferiority of the female gender only in order to supersede them.

The queen completes this process of self-definition by inscribing herself in prestigious male discourses. The divine right of kings and the theory of the king's two bodies are two of her favorites. As is well known, these discourses are related, but distinctive. Divine right envisions the monarch as God's anointed regent, from whom lesser beings descend in an orderly, vertical hierarchy of ever decreasing authority. A frequently used divine right metaphor represents the kingdom as a body, with the monarch as the head and subjects as the members of that body. In contrast, the idea of the king's two bodies originated in medieval theology and law, with the aim of establishing corporate perpetuity before the development of the modern idea of the state as an independent entity. As Marie Axton explains, lawyers in sixteenth-century England

> were formulating an idea of the state as a perpetual corporation, yet they were unable or unwilling to separate state and monarch. Their concept of the king's two bodies was an attempt to deal with a paradox: men died and the land endured; kings died; the crown survived; individual subjects died but subjects always remained to be governed. . . . For the purposes of law it was found necessary by 1561

> to endow the Queen with two bodies: a *body natural* and a *body politic.*
> . . . The body politic was supposed to be *contained within the natural*
> *body of the Queen.* . . . The Queen's natural body was subject to in-
> fancy, infirmity, error and old age; her body politic, created out of a
> combination of faith, ingenuity and practical expediency, was held to
> be unerring and immortal.[16]

Elizabeth's accession speech shows her early mastery of these two discourses. "Considering I am God's creature, ordained to obey His appointment, I will thereto yield. . . . And as I am but one body naturally considered, though by His permission a body politic to govern, so I shall desire you all, my lords . . . to be assistant to me, that I with my ruling and you with your service may make a good account to almighty God," she announces (51–52). On the subject of the undecided succession, Elizabeth responds (1566) to Parliament's demands that she name an heir with a sharp reminder: "A strange thing that the foot should direct the head in so weighty a cause, which cause hath been so diligently weighed by us for that it toucheth us more than them." At a later point in the same speech, she repeats, "Your petition is to deal in the limitation of the succession. At this present, it is not convenient, nor never shall be without some peril unto you and certain danger unto me. . . . But as soon as there may be a convenient time and that it may be done with least peril unto you, although never without great danger unto me, I will deal therein for your safety and offer it unto you as your prince and head, without request. For it is monstrous that the feet should direct the head" (96, 97–98).

The speech that most clearly demonstrates Elizabeth's subtle rhetorical mode of turning a perceived gender liability into an asset remains her famous oration at Tilbury, made on the battlefield after the defeat of the Spanish Armada. In this short address, she presents herself (twice) as a "weak" woman who, conflating her female virginity with the integrity of England's territory, also has the needed male strength to defend body and kingdom.[17] She becomes both the virgin in need of protection and the chivalrous male military hero who will provide that protection:

> I am come among you at this time . . . being resolved in the midst
> and heat of the battle to live and die amongst you all, to lay down for

my God and for my kingdom and for my people mine honor and my blood even in the dust. I know I have the body but of a weak and feeble woman, but I have the heart and stomach of a king and of a king of England too—and take foul scorn that Parma or any prince of Europe should dare to invade the borders of my realm. To the which rather than any dishonor shall grow by me, I myself will venter my royal blood; I myself will be your general, judge, and rewarder of your virtue in the field. (326)

The above examples demonstrate the strength of the argument that one of Elizabeth's major rhetorical strategies is to claim her femaleness in order to discard it, thus disarming her subjects and neutralizing their insecurities about female rule by attaching herself to the greater prestige of male heroism and kingship. Yet, because they have not taken into account the full and imaginative range of gendered subject positions available in Renaissance England, existing analyses have either misread or overlooked Elizabeth's appropriation of female positions and consequently have underestimated her reliance on female rhetorics of authority. Thus far I have examined examples from the queen's speeches in which she grounds her authority in her metaphysical and political position as the legitimate heir in a male dynasty, relying on locating herself within traditionally male discourses of divine right and military heroism. These discourses assume the superiority of abstract, symbolic systems like divine right and the king's two bodies to actual, embodied experience, a gendered hierarchy of values that Elizabeth in the above examples seems to accept totally when justifying her decisions, prohibitions, and commands. I now turn to an overlooked component in the queen's rhetoric of self-legitimation and argue for these claims as female.

IV

Elizabeth's first claim to a specifically female authority can be seen in her frequent biographical justifications of her actions and desires as emanating from her own *experience of life*. That her simple survival— of her mother's execution, of being declared illegitimate by her father, of the complicated plots to discredit her politically during the reigns of her siblings, of imprisonment, enforced religious conversion, smallpox, and forty-five years as a woman on the English throne—is in itself remarkable is a little-observed fact about Elizabeth I, but it is nonetheless crucial.[18]

Throughout her written texts, Elizabeth articulates a consciousness of herself as a survivor, one "whose life [God] hath miraculously preserved, at sundry times (beyond my merit) from a multitude of perils and dangers"(192). This self-definition corresponds to the representation of the queen, common at the beginning of her reign, as a Protestant savior of her people from the repression perpetrated by the Catholic queen, Elizabeth's sister, Mary I. In his *Acts and Monuments of the Martyrs,* for example, John Foxe paints Elizabeth as a hero of endurance, destined to deliver her people. Elizabeth becomes the queen who "after so long restrainment, so great dangers escaped, such blusterous storms overblown, so many injuries digested and wrongs sustained, by the mighty protection of our merciful God, to our no small comfort and commodity, hath been exalted and erected out of thrall to liberty, out of danger to peace and quietness, from dread to dignity, from misery to majesty, from mourning to ruling: briefly, of a prisoner made a princess, and placed in her throne royal, proclaimed now queen."[19] Elizabeth often employs this theme, inscribing herself as the embattled protagonist in a trajectory of deliverance. As quoted above, she rebukes the Commons' plea for her to marry and name a successor by invoking her heroic role in such a narrative: "I trust you likewise do not forget that by me you were delivered whilst you were hanging on the bough ready to fall into the mud—yea, to be drowned in the dung" (72). And in her 1585 speech on religion, she again reminds Parliament of her ability to survive perils: "I know no creature that breatheth whose life standeth hourly in more peril for [religion] than mine own, who entered not into my state without sight of manifold dangers of life and crown, as one that had the mightiest and greatest to wrestle with" (182).

But Elizabeth does not focus on the ways her ability to survive constitutes her heroic authority simply by presenting herself as the instrument of God's grace. She more frequently justifies her decisions as emanating from her own wisdom, wisdom that could be attained only from immersion in lived, personal experience. Comparing two of her most eloquent meditations on death helps to make the point.

As noted earlier, in the Armada speech (1588) the queen defines herself in the traditional rhetoric of masculine heroics as "being resolved in the midst and heat of the battle to live and die amongst you all, to lay down for my God and for my kingdom and for my people mine honor and my blood even in the dust" (326). The terms are those of the male heroics of action; the queen attributes her authority to the courage of willing self-sacrifice for relatively abstract causes: God and nation. These claims make an interesting contrast with the following, much more characteristic passage from her 1586 speech to Parliament regarding the appropriate treatment for the revealed treacheries of Mary, Queen of Scots:

> If by my death, other nations and kingdoms might truly say that this realm had attained an ever prosperous and flourishing estate, I would (I assure you) not desire to live, but gladly give my life to the end my death might procure you a better prince.
>
> And for your sakes it is that I desire to live, to keep you from a worse. For as for me, I assure you I find no great cause I should be fond to live; I take no such pleasure in it that I should much wish it, nor conceive such terror in death that I should greatly fear it. And yet I say not but if the stroke were coming, perchance flesh and blood would be moved with it and seek to shun it.
>
> *I have had good experience and trial of this world*: I know what it is to be a subject, what to be a sovereign; what to have good neighbors, and sometime meet evil willers. I have found treason in trust, seen great benefits little regarded, and instead of gratefulness, courses of purpose to cross.
>
> These former remembrances, present feeling, and future expectation of evils, I say, have made me think an evil is much the better the less while it endureth, and so, them happiest that are soonest hence. (192–93; emphasis added)

This passage implicitly exposes the negative values of the heroics of action (i.e., not fearing death) by transforming the meaning of courage: dying is easy; living is hard. "There needs no boding of my bane," Elizabeth tells Parliament in a wonderful line in 1563, after surviving smallpox; "I know now as well as I did before that I am mortal" (71). "And for your sakes it is that I desire to live," she explains in 1586 (193); and, in a later passage, "For it is not my desire to be or reign longer than my life and reign shall be for your good" (342). Survival, not death, constitutes the meaningful self-sacrifice.

There could be no more profound rejection of the male heroics of action than the queen's repeated refusal to privilege death. Interestingly, she often represents her ability to survive in explicitly female terms: "I am your anointed queen. I will never be by violence constrained to do anything. I thank God I am indeed endued with such qualities that if I were turned out of the realm in my petticoat, I were able to live in any place of Christendom" (97).

Elizabeth substantiates her claim for the heroics of survival by invoking the unique facts of her personal biography. Justifying her refusal to name a successor, she reminds Parliament early in her reign (1566) what she learned from occupying her vulnerable position as a subject next in line for the throne during the reign of her sister Mary: "I am sure there was not one of them that ever was a second person, as I have been, and have tasted of the practices against my sister, who I would to God were alive again. I had great occasions to hearken to their motions, of whom some of them are of the Common House. But when friends fall out truth doth appear, according to the old proverb, and were it not for my honor, their knavery should be known. There were occasions in me at that time: I stood in danger of my life, my sister was so incensed against me. I did differ from her in religion and I was sought for divers ways, and so shall never be my successor" (96). In a memorandum written after this speech, William Cecil tries valiantly to convey the substance of the queen's angry words to the full House of Commons. Interestingly, he picks up on her reasoning from personal experience in order to validate her claims. In what appears to be a last draft, for example, Cecil writes, "For she said she knew many causes and some of her own experience, having been a second person to a sister (the late queen meant) how perilous it was for her own person" (99).

When claiming the authority of lived experience, Elizabeth is quite concrete. As noted, her survival of the actual facts of her biography is adduced to justify her decisions. An interesting contrast to the longer passage (quoted above) from her 1586 speech on Mary, Queen of Scots, is a passage from a speech by James I, which he delivered in 1605 after the failure of the Gunpowder Plot. Speaking of the "daily tempest of innumerable dangers," James contends, "I amongst all other Kings have ever been subject unto them, not only ever since my birth, but even as I may justly say, before my birth; and while I was yet in my mother's belly: yet have I been exposed to two more special and greater dangers then all the rest. . . .Yet it pleased God to deliver me, as it were from the very brink of death, from the point of the dagger, and so to purge me by my thankful acknowledgement of so great a benefit."[20] As noted, Elizabeth also uses the trope of divine and wondrous delivery to authorize herself. But she is much more likely to stress her surviving of her troubles as a credential earned as well as granted: her process of reasoning, she labors to prove, stems directly, and so accurately, from specified events of her biography. Where Elizabeth is concrete, James is vague and general, citing his dangers as "the first of them, in the Kingdom where I was born, and passed the first part of my life: And the last of them here, which is the greatest."[21] Elizabeth argues and reasons as an active agent establishing her authority, partially by identifying with, rather than hierarchically distinguishing herself from, her subjects ("I have had good experience and trial of this world: I know what it is to be a subject, what to be a sovereign" [193]). In contrast, James's sole emphasis is upon the way his deliverances define him as unique. He presents himself as sui generis, a king among kings ("I amongst all other kings"). His authority, manifestly, is a fait accompli. Further, he represents himself passively, as a child, indeed as a fetus ("while I was yet in my mother's belly"), objectifying himself; he is marked as God's chosen, God's darling.

I would like to return to the idea that Elizabeth's self-legitimizing use of actual biographical experience situates her in a female subject position. Constance Jordan and Maureen Quilligan each have demonstrated that, in the Renaissance, the rhetorical recourse to lived experience constitutes an explicitly (characteristically) female claim to authority.[22] Jordan has shown, for example, the ways in which female empirical experience opposes itself to male symbolic (usually textual) systems that exclude women in feminist polemics throughout the sixteenth and seventeenth centuries, whether written by a woman or a man; indeed, she makes clear that many men occupied the rhetorical position designated female in debates about gender throughout the Renaissance.

Nevertheless, Elizabeth's reliance on these claims specifically relates her to other Renaissance women writers with whose works she was more than likely familiar.[23] In Marguerite de Navarre's *Heptameron* (1558), for example, authority of invention is granted to the mother figure, Oisille, "a widow with much experience of life."[24] And Quilligan has examined the ways in which Christine de Pizan constructs her *Book of the City of Ladies* (1403) around an opposition between the abstract, male-dominated canon of misogynist texts and the contrasting, empirical actualities of female (bodily) experience, what De Pizan herself calls "the natural behavior and character of women."[25]

Quilligan argues convincingly for Christine as "one of the first female writers to articulate what is specifically gendered about the female experience of history—what is in fact gendered *differently* from males." Christine neither seeks to overthrow the male textual tradition, nor to counter it with a female tradition, but to revise and expand it to include women. Her aim is not revolutionary, but corrective. Paradoxically, in order to locate the need for revision in the demonstrable falseness of male writers who exclude women in the first place, as well as to consolidate her own, lettered legitimacy, she "strives to establish her specific, female authority on alternative grounds to a merely scripted textual tradition," thus opposing "a prior, unscripted freedom" to "men's written laws."[26]

In the generic reading scene that begins *City of Ladies*, De Pizan locates the source of gender oppression not only in men's slander, but in women's surrender of the personal knowledge that comes from the actual, embodied experience of being female to the institutionalized and encoded male discursive constructions of woman. Encountering some of the classic male texts in this first scene, De Pizan is challenged by their misogyny to oppose her lived experience to their inscribed authority, though at first she fails to do so:

> And so I relied more on the judgement of others than on what I myself felt and knew. I was so transfixed in this line of thinking for such a long time that it seemed as if I were in a stupor. Like a gushing fountain, a series of authorities, whom I recalled one after another, came

to mind, along with their opinions on this topic [female inferiority].
And I finally decided that God formed a vile creature when he made
woman. . . . As I was thinking this, a great unhappiness and sadness
welled up in my heart, for I detested myself and the entire feminine
sex, as though we were monstrosities in nature.[27]

De Pizan learns that abdicating knowledge gained from personal experience and judgment that contradicts dominant narratives results in
self-hatred, which in turn allows oppression to continue unchecked.
Thus enlightened, she is able to acknowledge the extent of her dependence upon, and participation in, the male textual tradition, in which
she then boldly intervenes, seeking radically to revise existing assumptions.

In a similarly pluralistic manner, Elizabeth I both opposes and draws
upon traditional female and traditional male rhetorics of authority, distinctively valuing both. This rhetorical strategy forms the basis of my argument that the queen seeks to monopolize all dominant gendered
subject positions in her texts of self-legitimation. This process as a
whole becomes visible when some examples from her speeches that
thus far have been viewed separately are examined in conjunction with
one another.

Elizabeth's marital status continues to trouble and perplex both the
international community and her own people for at least half of her
reign. In fact it is scarcely an exaggeration to say that a large chunk of
her reign is in effect framed, at the beginning by letters and petitions
begging her to marry and around the late middle by letters and pam-
phlets begging her not to.[28] In procrastinating about marriage and
naming a successor, the queen recognizes the anomalous powers of
choice and definition uniquely available to her in a culture that (offi-
cially at least) silences women. Responding to Parliament's recurring
plea that she declare a successor, she upsets the conventions of gender
by asserting her right to her own desire:

> God, who hath hitherto therein preserved and led me by the hand,
> will not now of His goodness suffer me to go alone.
>   For the other part, the manner of your petition I do well like of
> and take in good part, because that it is simple and containeth no
> limitation of place or person. If it had been otherwise, I must needs

have misliked it very much and thought it in you a very great pre-
sumption, being unfitting and altogether unmeet for you to require
them that may command, or those to appoint whose parts are to desire, or such to bind and limit whose duties are to obey, or to take
upon you to draw my love to your liking or frame my will to your
fantasies. For a guerdon constrained and a gift freely given can never
agree together. (57)

Elizabeth also asserts her right to self-definition. Regarding her single
state she contends, "[I]t is most true that at this day I stand free from
any other meaning that either I have had in times past or have at this
present" (57). Interestingly, Elizabeth does not justify her (as a
woman, appropriated) rights to define and desire by describing herself
as the exceptional female member of a male dynastic system; although
she does refer to God's will, she authorizes her decision to remain single primarily from the facts of her biography, citing her status as a survivor. Specifically, in the following passage from a 1559 speech, she
discusses her vulnerability during the reign of Mary I to being impli-
cated in plots to overthrow her sister, and Mary's consequent constant
suspicion of her:

> And to the first part, I may say unto you that from my years of un-
> derstanding, sith I first had consideration of myself to be born a
> servitor of almighty God, I happily chose this kind of life in which I
> yet live, which I assure you for mine own part hath hitherto best con-
> tented myself and I trust hath been most acceptable to God. From
> the which if either ambition of high estate offered to me in marriage
> by the pleasure and appointment of my prince [i.e., Queen Mary]
> . . . or if the eschewing of the danger of mine enemies; or the avoid-
> ing of the peril of death, whose messenger or rather continual
> watchman, the prince's indignation, was not little time daily before
> mine eyes, by whose means although I know, or justly may suspect,
> yet will not now utter; or if the whole cause were in my sister her-
> self, I will not now burden her therewith, because I will not charge
> the dead. If any of these, I say, could have drawn or dissuaded me
> from this kind of life, I had not now remained in this estate wherein
> you see me; but constant have always continued in this determina-
> tion. (56, 57)

In the same speech, the queen directly opposes dynastic claims to bodily ones, in this case fear of the consequences of pregnancy and childbirth: "And albeit it might please almighty God to continue me still in this mind to live out of the state of marriage, yet it is not to be feared but He will so work in my heart and in your wisdoms as good provision by His help may be made in convenient time, whereby the realm shall not remain destitute of an heir that may be a fit governor, and peradventure more beneficial to the realm than such offspring as may come of me. For although I be never so careful of your well-doings, and mind ever so to be, *yet may my issue grow out of kind* and become, perhaps, ungracious" (58; emphasis added). While Elizabeth clearly refers here to the possibility of usurpation by her children and so civil war, the pun on "grow out of kind" (become unnatural) could also refer, however subliminally, to the possibility of physical deformity. With this reading, Elizabeth oddly allies herself with the uncertainties and infirmities of the body natural, as a kind of counter-claim to the body politic.[29]

The queen again confronts an angry Parliament demanding resolution of the marriage and succession question seven years later, in 1566. Arguing once more against the concerns of the Lords and Commons for an orderly transition that would prevent civil war in the event of her death, Elizabeth does to some extent rely on the standard tropes of the divine right of kings in the body politic ("A strange thing that the foot should direct the head in so weighty a cause, which cause hath been so diligently weighed by us for that it toucheth us more than them" [96]). But again the metaphorical body of the kingdom takes second place both to the queen's natural body and to her particular experience of life. As we have seen, she angrily accuses Parliament of a kind of political thoughtlessness in this speech, arguing, "I am sure there was not one of them that ever was a second person, as I have been, and have tasted of the practices against my sister, who I would to God were alive again" (96). This speech ends by repeating its earlier evocation of divine right and the body politic ("For it is monstrous that the feet should direct the head" [98]); but, once again, this rhetoric is countered by a striking image of the queen's body natural, which, as in her earlier speech about pregnancy, evokes the possibility of marriage as a bodily / sexual violation: "I am your anointed queen. I will never be by violence constrained to do anything. I thank God I am indeed endued with such qualities that if I were turned out of the realm in my petticoat, I were able to live in any place of Christendom" (97). These remarks, which so pointedly evoke the queen's femaleness, immediately follow a statement in which, adapting the rhetoric of the male heroics of action, she defies death and attaches her heroism to her father's: "As for my own part, I care not for death, for all men are mortal; and though I be a woman, yet I have as good a courage answerable to my place as ever my father had. I am your anointed queen. . . ." (97). Taken as a whole, the passage reveals how in her speeches Elizabeth both makes dynastic claims and dissociates herself from them. Further, juxtaposing the allusions to bodily violation in this speech with the fears articulated in the earlier speech on succession grants weight to the hypothesis that Elizabeth's ominous, reiterated references to "some peril unto you and certain danger unto me" (97) point to a desire to avoid death in childbirth as one major reason, along with fears about civil war and subordinating herself to a husband, for her refusal to marry or to name a successor.

V

I do not disagree with existing interpretations of Elizabeth I that demonstrate how she constructs her power as extending vertically downward from God through her sovereign body to her subjects as members of that body. Nevertheless I find these analyses incomplete, and so distorting. I argue that, while to some extent the queen privileges male subjectivity, in her speeches she also constructs a position for herself outside of the male dynastic system; and that this position, which relies on what I am terming a female rhetoric of legitimation, is equally responsible for the effectiveness of her self-creation as a ruler. To conclude I offer one additional argument: in her speeches Elizabeth often constructs her authority as a dialogue, involving reciprocity between her subjects and herself. This particular theme, which changes and grows throughout her reign, becomes evident—when marriage ceases to be an issue—in the statements she makes about love.

In terms of chronology, this development contrasts interestingly with the cult of Elizabeth which, mystifying and idealizing the queen's virginity, flourishes at the end of her reign, when she is no longer able to procreate. For as many scholars have shown, the iconographical and literary representations that characterize the cult's productions emphasize the queen's position as unattainable beloved in relation to her male courtiers, resembling in this structural sense the female object of desire in a Petrarchan sonnet: adored and sought for, but never won. It is argued that this conception of Elizabeth as self-contained, an icon, unmoved but moving, desired but never desiring, allows for the anomaly of female rule at the top by providing a familiar symbolic structure of courtship in which men could function politically as suitors.[30]

There is a great deal of evidence from the period to sustain this argument. In his elegy for Elizabeth, for example, Francis Bacon praises her for cleverly allowing herself "to be wooed and courted . . . for certain it is that these dalliances detracted but little from her fame and nothing at all from her majesty, and neither weakened her power nor sensibily hindered her business." Bacon finds it particularly shrewd that Elizabeth, as he puts it, "allows of amorous admiration but prohibits desire."[31] The speeches, however, provide equally strong evidence of a simultaneous but contrasting trajectory, one in which the queen presents herself increasingly as accessible and dependent upon her subjects.

In her early speeches Elizabeth relies heavily on inscribing herself in male symbolic systems like divine right that do indeed represent her as supernaturally and uniquely empowered, with the corollary that her subjects' role is to submit and obey her, just as her role is to submit and obey God. "I am God's creature, ordained to obey His appointment. . . . I am but one body naturally considered, though by His permission a body politic to govern," she announces in her accession speech (51– 52), continuing, "my meaning is to require of you all nothing more but faithful hearts in such service as from time to time shall be in your powers towards the preservation of me and this commonwealth" (52). As noted, in Elizabeth's early speeches that focus on the issue of her marriage and the succession, she adamantly relies on divine right, it "being unfitting and altogether unmeet for you to require them that may command" (57). Referring in 1563 to "the princely seat and kingly throne wherein God (though unworthy) hath constituted me" (70), she reminds Parliament "that by me you were delivered whilst you were hanging on the bough ready to fall into the mud—yea, to be drowned in the dung" (72). Observing in a holograph draft opening fragment (1566), "I marvel not much that bridleless colts do not know their rider's hand, whom bit of kingly rein did never snaffle yet" (93), she reiterates that "it is monstrous that the feet should direct the head" (98). Her promises to marry disbelieved, the queen retorts with outrage when Parliament attaches its demands to her request for a subsidy: "I did send them answer by my Council I would marry, although of mine own disposition I was not inclined thereunto. But that was not accepted nor credited, although spoken by their prince. And yet I used so many words that I could say no more. And were it not now I had spoken those words, I would never speak them again. I will never break the word of a prince spoken in public place for my honor sake" (95). Rank, hierarchy, obedience, command as they are defined in traditional theological and political discourses: these are all major themes in Elizabeth's speeches during the first decade of her reign.

The queen's early attempts to render orthodox her unconventional authority (often a defensive response to the demand that she marry) undergoes an extraordinary transformation during her career as monarch. The transition from her strict construction of a divine right hierarchy following the lines of the great chain of being to a conception of mutual dependence among her subjects and herself can be seen in her address to Parliament in 1576.

According to Neale, Elizabeth's 1576 speech occurs at the end of a comparatively uneventful Parliament and seems to have no immediate or specific political or diplomatic purpose. "She wrote it, apparently, because she wanted to," so Allison Heisch concludes.[32] The queen's last major courtship with D'Alencon is ahead of her, so her potential marriage and the succession are still issues seventeen years into her reign. But in 1576 she is forty-three years old and known to her people; the tone and technique of her oration have altered demonstrably. She is still procrastinating about marriage and citing her (implicitly) superior biographical experience in order to justify her non-decisions:

> Mine experience teacheth me to be no fonder of these vain delights than reason would, nor further to delight in things uncertain than may seem convenient. But let good heed be taken lest in reaching too

far after future good, you peril not the present, or begin to quarrel and fall by dispute together by the ears before it be decided who shall wear my crown. (170)

Yet, not only is her tone more gentle than it is in the speeches of the 1560s, the queen also empathizes with her subjects, rather than chastising them:

> I will not deny but I might be thought the indifferentist judge in this respect, that shall not be at all when these things be fulfilled: which none beside myself can speak in all this company. Misdeem not of my words as though I sought what heretofore to others hath been granted. I intend it not. My brains be too thin to carry so tough a matter, although I trust God will not in such haste cut off my days but that, according to your own desert and my desire, I may provide some good way for your security (170–71).

According to your own desert and my desire. This newly unconflicted linkage of her desires with the welfare of her subjects becomes clear if we contrast the passage just quoted with the following excerpt from a speech addressing the same issues ten years earlier, when she in effect dares her subjects to question her will, thus pointing to their doing so as an outrage:

> Was I not born in the realm? Were my parents born in any foreign country? Is there any cause I should alienate myself from being careful over this country? Is not my kingdom here? Whom have I oppressed? Whom have I enriched to others' harm? What turmoil have I made in this commonwealth, that I should be suspected to have no regard to the same? How have I governed since my reign? I will be tried by envy itself. I need not to use many words, for my deeds do try me. (95)

In earlier years, Elizabeth relies upon distinguishing herself from her subjects through the superiority of both her rank and her experience. Indeed she often points out the disparities between herself and her subjects by insisting on the fact that, being the monarch, she has more to lose than they do. She continually alludes to a time when naming a successor "may be done with least peril unto you, although never without great danger unto me" (98). In 1559, commenting again on the ever troubling marriage question, Elizabeth observes, "For I know that this matter toucheth me much nearer than it doth you all, who if the worst happen can lose but your bodies. But if I take not that convenient care that it behoveth me to have therein, I hazard to lose both body and soul" (71).

Alluding to divine right, the above quotation implies that there are three protagonists in Elizabeth's definition of her relationship with her subjects: herself, her subjects as a body, and God. As she reconsiders and redefines her authority throughout her reign, God takes a progressively and demonstrably lesser role, just as the hierarchical distance between herself and her subjects begins to level out into reciprocal connectedness. This process first becomes noticeable in the 1576 speech. Her theme has become one of gratitude rather than antagonism, and the mutually beneficial relation with her subjects that Elizabeth outlines is attributable to God. Noticeably, however, in her expressions of gratitude, she no longer distinguishes herself from her subjects, but begins to identify herself with them in relation to God:

> I cannot attribute this hap and good success to my device without detracting much from the divine Providence, nor challenge to my own commendation what is only due to His eternal glory. My sex permits it not, or if it might be in this kind, yet find I no impeachment why to persons of more base estate the like proportion should not be allotted. . . . These seventeen years God hath both prospered and protected you with good success under my direction, and I nothing doubt but the same maintaining hand will guide you still and bring you to the ripeness of perfection. . . . The best way, I suppose, *for you and me* were by humble prayers to require of God that not in weighing but in perfect weight, in being not in seeming, we may wish the best and further it with our abilities. (168–69; emphasis added)

In 1576, then, God receives the ultimate credit for the prosperity of England. The attribution to God must of course remain in the speeches, and the queen's expressions of gratitude to God never disappear. Yet, the 1576 speech provides evidence that Elizabeth has begun to identify lovingly with her subjects. No longer speaking as a remote, inaccessible object of dread and desire, she eventually develops a view of her relationship with her subjects as a dialogue, a process of reciprocity. Responding to complaints about monopolies in the famous Golden Speech (1601), for example, she says, "Of myself I must say this: I never was any greedy, scraping grasper, nor a strait fast-holding prince, nor yet a waster. My heart was never set on any worldly goods, but only for my subjects' good. *What you bestow on me, I will not hoard it up, but receive it to bestow on you again*" (337–38; emphasis added).

In the Golden Speech, the queen's observations on her loving relationship with her subjects appear in an economic context; the discussion centers on subsidies and monopolies. It is useful to compare her handling of these conjoined issues with that of the two most prominent male monarchs who precede and succeed her, Henry VIII and James I.

In his Christmas Eve speech of 1545 (his only recorded parliamentary speech), Henry thanks Parliament for the subsidies granted him and uses the occasion to exhort his subjects to religious "toleration." On the one hand, it is probable that Elizabeth learned the political effectiveness of discussing love of her subjects from the strength of her father's pronouncements. On the other, it is fascinating to observe how differently father and daughter treat this same theme. Referring to himself as "he that setteth more by your loving hearts, than by your substance," Henry declares,

> Now, sithence I find such kindness on your part toward me, I can not choose but love and favor you, affirming that no prince in the world more favoreth his subjects than I do you, nor no subjects or commons more love and obey their sovereign lord, than I perceive you do me, for whose defense my treasure shall not be hidden, nor if necessity require my person shall not be unadventured: yet although I with you and you with me be in this perfect love and concord, this friendly amity cannot continue, except both you my lords temporal, and you my lords spiritual, and you my loving subjects, study and take pain to amend one thing, which surely is amiss and far out of order, to the which I most heartily require you, which is that charity and concord is not amongst you, but discord and dissention beareth rule in every place. . . . Amend these crimes I exhort you, and set forth God's word, both by true preaching and good example giving, or else I whom God hath appointed his Vicar and high minister here will see these divisions extinct, and these enormities corrected.[33]

The hierarchy here is quite clear: Henry is God's appointed minister. He is empowered well beyond his subjects and will not hesitate to use that power against them if they refuse to obey his commands. Gratitude ("I can not choose but love and favor you") is conditional ("yet although I with you and you with me be in this perfect concord . . . this friendly amity can not continue, except . . .) and is quickly followed by threat ("Amend these crimes . . . or else").

Where Henry threatens directly, James reflects pompously. In a 1609 speech, for example, James embeds a request for subsidies in a discourse dwelling on the divine right of kings. Far from alluding to any possibility of reciprocity between himself and his subjects, James lectures Parliament on the nature of monarchical power, reminding them that, like God, kings "have the power to exalt low things and abase high things, and make of their subjects like men at Chess." Whereas Henry and Elizabeth describe their special relationships with God, James is himself god-like. Ironically James's pedantic need to explain kingship weakens his request for money, indicating his lack of true confidence:

> And though in a sort this may seem to be my particular; yet it can not be divided from the general good of the Commonwealth; For the King that is *Parens Patriae,* tells you of his wants. . . . For if the King want, the State wants, and therefore the strengthening of the King is the preservation and the standing of the State; And woe be to him that divides the weal of the King from the weal of the Kingdom. . . . For if you part without the repairing of my State in some reasonable sort, what can the world think, but that the evil will my Subjects bear unto me, hath bred a refuse? And ye can never part so, without apprehending that I am distasted with your behaviour, and yet to be in fear of my displeasure.[34]

Toward the end of her reign, Elizabeth begins to view the loving dialogue between herself and her subjects not merely as a manifestation of her power, but as a source of it. Whereas Henry and James each rely almost exclusively on divine right, Elizabeth often opposes the claims of relationship with her subjects to the claims of dynasty; even more radically, she privileges the former, as the syntax of the following passage from the Golden Speech makes clear:

Mr. Speaker, we perceive your coming is to present thanks unto me; know it I accept with no less joy than your loves can desire to offer such a present, and more esteem it than any treasure or riches (for that we know how to prize), but loyalty, love, and thanks I count invaluable. *And though God hath raised me high, yet this I count the glory of my crown—that I have reigned with your loves. This makes I do not so much rejoice that God hath made me to be a queen, as to be a queen over so thankful a people.* (340; emphasis added)

The reciprocity enters in with Elizabeth's recognition of the mutual gratitude at the heart of the process of exchange she describes.

While Henry also asserts his gratitude toward his subjects, in contrast to his daughter he simultaneously reasserts the vertical hierarchical structure that places the king squarely above his subjects, making absolutely clear who is boss. In further contrast, when James is considering love or gratitude between monarch and subjects, he tends to dilate upon himself as an object of his subjects' desire: "these blessings which God hath jointly with my Person sent unto you." James's self-conception here recalls the last words of Marlowe's Tamburlaine, who, dying, mourns not his own loss of the world, but his subjects' loss of him : "My body feels, my soul doth weep to see, / Your sweet desires deprived my company" (5.3.220–21).[35]

Neither Henry nor James approaches the conception of mutuality, the loving reciprocal exchange that Elizabeth creates in her late speeches. While she retains divine right, toward the end of her reign she reduces her emphasis on it. What results is a virtual redefinition of the center of power, represented not as a series of relationships based on dominance, submission, and unequal wills, but as a dialogue rooted in gratefully acknowledged mutual dependencies between subjects and monarch.

But does the queen really feel these things, or is she simply a master politician, shrewdly calculating what would sell? The question of the genuineness of Elizabeth's feelings, or even of the level of them, is in fact not critical to an inquiry into the gendered terms in which she constructs her authority. Yet it is possible to speculate. If we allow Elizabeth I to be a complex person, not necessarily instead of, but as well as, an all-powerful icon, it becomes clear that throughout her life emotional intimacy was barely, if ever, safely accessible to her. Being queen was for her more than a full-time job. Thus when she writes in 1586 that

> although there liveth not any that may more justly acknowledge themselves infinitely bound unto God than I, whose life He hath miraculously preserved at sundry times (beyond my merit) from a multitude of perils and dangers; yet is not that the cause for which I count myself the deepliest bound to give Him my humblest thanks, or to yield Him greatest recognition, but this which I shall tell you hereafter, which will deserve the name of wonder if rare things and seldom seen be worthy of account. Even this it is: that as I came to the crown with the willing hearts of my subjects, so do I now after twenty-eight years' reign perceive in you no diminution of goodwills, which if haply I should want, well might I breathe, but never think I lived (192)

it is quite possible to imagine the gratification she describes as being neither a sentimental nor a mystified response, but a response to reality as she experienced it.

VI

Representing existence as struggle and achievement, the heroics of action and the heroics of endurance taken together offer aspiring protagonists severe and formidable choices. As I discussed in the prologue, the accomplishment of heroic identity would seem to consist either of killing and dominating, thus courageously risking death and defeat (male); or suffering and submitting, thus patiently enduring pain and death (female, male, or both). To kill or die well: these are the distilled elements of heroism.

There remains one alternative to these alarming options: survival. Heroic survival can range from witty triumph over obstacles to resigned acceptance of limitations and can appear as a manifestation of both the heroics of action and the heroics of endurance. Thus the surviving hero can occupy both male and female subject positions. I hope to have demonstrated that in her speeches Elizabeth I makes survival a key component of her heroic identity and associates it predominantly with the female. In what follows I will examine the textual strategies of women writers who become heroic survivors without also being queens.

THREE

Gender, Genre, and History: Female Heroism in Seventeenth-Century Autobiography

I

Like the projections of male heroism produced by Marlowe and Jonson, Elizabeth I constructs her heroic persona by seeking omnipotence through a rhetorical monopoly of dominant gendered subject positions. In contrast to Marlowe's and Jonson's fluid representations of fictional male heroes, Elizabeth's are those of an actual, embodied woman; rather than repressing femaleness in a disingenuous denial of its value, she takes advantage of the special prestige of both male and female subject positions without consistently privileging either. As any Renaissance or early modern woman would need to do, she makes a continuing, self-conscious effort to defend her disturbing presence in the public realm; unlike any other woman, though, she does so with complete assurance of her privileged identity and her consequent right to occupy public space. The radical aspect of Elizabeth's gendering of female heroic agency therefore consists in its confidence, and that confidence resides in the anomalous fact that she is a queen.

In an extraordinary utopian text entitled *The Description of a New World, Called the Blazing-World* (1668), Margaret Cavendish, Duchess of Newcastle, locates her heroic agency very precisely in the fact that she is not—nor can she ever be—an anointed queen. While she struggles with fantasies of royalty and absolutism, she recognizes that her subjectivity must be self-created and exist apart from the public realm.[1] "I am not Covetous, but as Ambitious as ever any of my Sex was, is, or can be," she states candidly, "which is the cause That though I cannot be Henry the Fifth, or Charles the Second; yet, I will endeavor to be, Margaret the First: and though I have neither Power, Time, nor Occasion, to be a great Conqueror, like Alexander or Caesar; yet, rather than not be Mistress of a World, since Fortune and the Fates would give me none, I have made One of my own" (prologue, "To All Noble and Worthy Ladies").[2]

In the passage just quoted, Cavendish simultaneously preserves and defies the conditions of traditional male heroism. On the one hand, her catalog of admired heroes, whom to her regret she cannot emulate, is composed entirely of male sovereigns and military conquerors; on the other hand, she insists on her ability to imagine herself as a hero, particularly as the hero of her own life, her own inner, private world. Indeed the entirety of *Blazing-World* can be seen as a self-conscious, ambivalent representation of female heroic agency, which the text divides between a powerful Empress and her brilliant advisor, pointedly named the Duchess of Newcastle. Together the two women roam freely among worlds and, with the aid of a fantastic group of animal-men, perform a series of astounding feats. Although she names the advisor rather than the sovereign after herself, Cavendish claims both figures as "parts of my Mind. . . . [Y]ou may perceive that my ambition is not only to be Empress but Authoress of a whole world" (epilogue). In short she is a split subject. At the end she summarizes her complex engagement with heroism by simultaneously claiming and abjuring the traditional hero's quest for omnipotence:

> I esteeming peace before war, wit before policy, honesty before beauty; instead of the figures of Alexander, Caesar, Hector, Achilles, Nestor, Ulysses, Helen, etc. [I] chose rather the figure of Honest Margaret Newcastle, which now I would not change for all this Terrestrial World; and if any should like the World I have made, and be willing to be my Subjects, they may imagine themselves such, and they are such, I mean in their Minds, Fancies, or Imaginations; but if they cannot endure to be Subjects, they may create Worlds of their own, and Govern themselves as they please. (epilogue)

Just as she does at the beginning of *Blazing-World,* in its conclusion Cavendish designates the private realm as her kingdom, imagined as a separate but equal sphere. The private realm offers space for an alternative and, she suggests, superior mode of heroism, which as the entire text makes clear is specifically imagined as female. Yet, in defining this realm, she borrows the descriptive heroic terms associated with public life. Further, Cavendish's designation of a separated private zone as the appropriate sphere for women takes the contradictory and ironic form of a public declaration. Despite her insistence that self-assertion for non-royal women can take place only if they construct themselves as queens of an imagined private space, Cavendish publishes *Blazing-World,* directly addressing her ambivalent self-definitions to an expected readership.

Indeed, the autobiographical passages in *Blazing-World* indicate precisely the way many women writers construct their heroic agency as an embattled negotiation of changing boundaries between public and private realms. In the following discussion I explore this phenomenon as it emerges in the late seventeenth century, when increasing numbers of women begin to engage in autobiographical writing, contributing noticeably to a genre in which, perforce, they create themselves as heroes of their own lives. I argue that in these life accounts, tension between the fluidity in much thinking about gender in the Renaissance and the increasingly well-defined discourses and material practices that systematically exclude women from public action and self-expression is acutely felt. Consequently female heroism emerges as always and already contradictory and problematic.

II

Largely excluded from the political arena and the professions, early modern women did not add to the accounts men wrote of their public lives and the development of their careers. When a woman wished to assert herself as a member of the community whose experience was worth recording, she was largely confined to the family history: her role as daughter, wife, and mother. Second, in the period surrounding the Civil War, many sectarian women published accounts of their religious experiences—visions, ecstasies, conversions, and dangerous evangelical journeys—that exempted them from traditional sexual arrangements as well as from the social and moral taboos against female self-expression.[3] In this chapter I focus on more conventional women who, unprotected by religious or political discourses that define them as exceptions, nevertheless undertake to write their autobiographies. Along with not being queens, the women with whom I am concerned are neither saints, mystics, nor proselytizers; rather they are traditional wives and mothers who, in the late seventeenth century, begin not simply to record the deeds of their male relatives, but to explore their secular identities and experiences in autobiographical form.

When the modern conventions of autobiography as a distinctively personal, secular, and introspective literary form begin to coalesce during the British Restoration, traditional wives and mothers can at once be recognized among the liveliest, most imaginative contributors to the evolving genre.[4] Viewed in terms of the early development of modern autobiography, the four women whose self-created heroism is the subject of this chapter—Margaret Cavendish, the Duchess of Newcastle (1625–1674); Anne, Lady Halkett (1623–1699); Ann, Lady Fanshawe (1625–1680); and Alice Thornton (1626/7–1706/7)—immediately sense the literary opportunity to construct themselves as social personalities. Rather than the articulation of their personal experience of the supernatural, or as passive recorders of genealogy and observers of men's deeds, what these women depict are their relations with other people and their actions within a social world of contemporary events. Although they are all pious, they do not seek to transcend what is experienced as the confinement of their bodies, but rather to embody and enact their spirituality in sexual relationships and social life.

Several reasons enabling these women to overcome the cultural injunction against female self-expression to the point of asserting the value of their individual secular experiences in autobiographical form immediately suggest themselves. In general the idea of an authentic, inner self, a realm of privacy in which women could claim some authority, is beginning to be publicly recognized and valued in the mid- to late seventeenth century.[5] Second, as several scholars have argued, autobiographical writing has few exacting formal conventions and can appear in different kinds of texts; women writers often excel when generic boundaries are construed as fluid and flexible.[6] Third, as is the case with three out of the four texts under consideration, secular autobiographies by both women and men tend to remain unpublished before the eighteenth century, so women autobiographers during the Restoration need not feel that they are asserting themselves scandalously in public.[7]

Finally and, as I will argue, most importantly, all four of these women live through the English Civil War, a period of social chaos that liberates them from many of the ordinary constrictions of gender ideology.

Thrust into the public arena by the Civil War, all four women are brave enough to write their autobiographies; yet each constructs her identity and experience as problematic. As Sidonie Smith and others contend, the making and remaking of a female self in autobiography emerges from "the dialogic engagement with the ideology of sexual difference promoted in the discourse of her time." For women in early modern England, a self-assertive engagement with "the overpowering expectations and assumptions of womanhood made by seventeenth-century society" inevitably results in division and conflict.[8] It is precisely the felt conflict between self-effacement and self-assertion that emerges from the attempt to navigate the boundaries between private and public lives which gives shape to women's autobiographical texts and characterizes their troubled heroism.

Interestingly, the self-divisions that distinguish female heroism are congenial with certain generic components of autobiography which exist regardless of the author's gender. Felicity Nussbaum argues that from the time modern autobiography is first conceptualized as a genre in early modern England, it projects a goal of the truthful recounting of the lives of individuals engaged in "autonomous and continuous self-fashionings." These expectations of coherently evolving self-creation coincide with "traces of new ideological assumptions" that include the belief that "the private inner 'self,' somehow more authentic than the public one, will be marked by more fluctuations and vacillations than the public. . . . Thus there is an assumption of a real and pregiven person behind the text." However, the autobiographer's claims to truth and authority in the recreation of a coherent selfhood are inevitably compromised: the author's subjectivity is generically divided into narrator and object of narration—the "I" of the subject matter and the "I" who speaks.[9] As critic Georges Gusdorf observes, because the autobiographer must assume, for example, the reliability of memory, the "impartiality of the self to itself," and the ability successfully to merge the present with the past in a single narrative framework, he or she "take(s) for granted the very thing that is in question," a gap between public and private intention that explains the puzzlement and ambivalence of the genre.[10]

Nussbaum contends that "by declaring [a] divided self textually, autobiography renders self-division increasingly commonplace and natural." Autobiography therefore participates in producing "an individual who believes she or he is the source and center of meaning."[11] Throughout this study I have defined the heroic as the location in the text where meanings inhere. Early modern women's autobiographical writing makes an important contribution not only to the developing genre, but also to a significant future trajectory for both male and female heroism. In what follows I will explore the ways the material practices and historical circumstances in which these women autobiographers are situated contribute to the transformations of heroism.

III

Countering the claims to truth and coherence made by modern autobiography and its critics, Nussbaum contends that "secular autobiographical narratives display multiple and serial subject positions that may not add up to a coherent self."[12] Margaret Cavendish's *A True Relation of My Birth, Breeding, and Life* (1656) is a perfect example of such a text.[13] Among the four women autobiographers considered here, Cavendish is in several important ways an exception. Like the other women, she is an upper-class Anglican and Royalist; the English Civil War ruptures the stable social and emotional world in which she has been brought up, filling her life with chaos and a variety of experiences that, in all likelihood, would otherwise have remained completely unavailable to her. Unlike the other three women, however, she never becomes a mother; nor is she a widow at the time she writes. She composes *A True Relation* while exiled in Antwerp with her husband, William Cavendish, the Marquis of Newcastle, who, in Virginia Woolf's words, "had led the King's forces to disaster with indomitable courage but little skill."[14] Cavendish is also the only one among these women who writes with the conscious intent of publication and, indeed, her autobiography, along with many other writings of hers, is published during her lifetime. Rather than composing as the others do, with her youth, her marriage, the Civil War, and the fear of indiscretion safely behind her, Cavendish abjures the organizing principle of hindsight, choosing instead to write, as it were, from the eye of the storm. As a result, although the challenges and problems of female heroism remain unresolved in her narrative, they are articulated with an immediacy that is unusually poignant and clear.

Not surprisingly, Cavendish's narrative and personal conflicts center on female agency: issues of independence, power, responsibility, and freedom of choice. As several critics have noted, she begins and ends her autobiography by defining herself in terms of her relations with others. In a frequently cited article, Mary Mason argues that Cavendish's narration presents a model of female autobiography, in which women consistently "record and dramatize self-realization . . . through the recognition of another"; and, according to Mason, Cavendish establishes "a pattern of alterity-equality in her depiction of her relationship with her husband" (235, 232).[15] But Cavendish's sense of attachment is in fact overwhelmed in her account by a more pressing sense of problematic uniqueness. It is true that her claim to attention as a daughter and a wife provides the rhetorical framework for her narrative (275, 318); yet her descriptions of her relations with others emerge not as a central, but as a subordinate element in the more compelling representation of her singularity. As an alter ego William Cavendish cuts a feeble, shadowy figure in *A True Relation,* never coming alive as a personality and making only brief, unconvincing appearances as an idealized moral character and as a writer whose abilities supposedly exceed those of his wife (306–7).[16] What does emerge from the account is not a personality who defines herself through relationship, but rather a troubled, complex, and indecisive shaping intelligence, whose narration can be characterized more usefully by the author's persistent ambivalence.

At one point, in an erratic burst of candor, Cavendish announces both a competitive desire to excel and an independent wish to control her own destiny: "I think it no crime to wish myself the exactest of Nature's works, my thread of life the longest, my Chain of Destiny the strongest, my mind the peaceblest; my life the pleasantest, my death the easiest, and the greatest saint in heaven; also to do my endeavour, so far as honour and honesty doth allow of, to be the highest on Fortune's Wheel, and to hold the Wheel from turning, if I can. And if it be commendable to wish another's good, it were a sin not to wish my own" (315).

But the natural self-regard and confident joy in singularity this passage expresses is not sustained in *A True Relation*. Indeed Cavendish is incapable of asserting herself without coming to a painful impasse. The narrative effect of her conflict between self-assertion and self-denial can best be disentangled by observing her repeated attempts to define herself not merely in terms of her personal attachments, but rather according to an early modern ideal of femininity, in which relations with others form a single element in a composite of prescribed character traits, including, along with subordination and obedience, modesty, chastity, shyness, gentleness, innocence, and silence.[17] These traits permeate Cavendish's idealized portrait of her mother, whom she memorializes as exquisitely beautiful, retiring, and even-tempered, a woman who, in educating her daughters, stressed the importance of moral character not as conjoined with, but at the expense of, discipline and skill (279–80). Indeed Cavendish absorbs this cultural ideal of the female so intensely that she goes on to represent herself as (with the exception of beauty, which she disavows) the embodiment of these qualities.

Yet Cavendish proves as unable to commit herself to the self-effacement required by culturally prescribed female behavior as she is to recognize and accept the challenge of an emerging ideology of individualism. Attempting to seem modest, for example, she often assures us that she is bashful to the point of foolishness: "I durst neither look up with my eyes, nor speak, nor be any way sociable, insomuch as I was thought a natural fool," she explains, in a purportedly self-critical account of her behavior as a young lady at court (287). But her girlish modesty turns out to be foolish wisdom: "Neither do I find my bashfulness riseth so often in blushes, as contracts my spirits to a chill paleness," she confides later (300), betraying a rather disintegrated preoccupation with the advantages her shyness lends to her physical appearance; indeed it is this very shyness that wins the love of the Marquis. But Cavendish does not simply disguise unacknowledged self-idealization as self-deprecation. She also does the opposite, namely, subverting her own claims to achievement or ambition with denial and self-contempt. Shortly after the passage quoted above, in which she exults in her uniqueness, she confesses to the reader in a moving and forthright paragraph the actual intensity of her ambition for fame which, "even if it be a vanity" (317), she nevertheless desires above all things. On the same page, clearly wishing to appear more "silent, chaste, and obedient," she reassures the reader that her deepest instinct is actually to "willingly exclude myself, so as never to see the face of any creature but my Lord as long as I live, enclosing myself like an anchorite, wearing a frieze gown, tied with a chord about my waist" (317). But earlier she had elaborated her love of dressing up in fashion designs of her own invention, "for I always took delight in a singularity" (312). Furthermore, despite "being addicted from my childhood to contemplation rather than conversation" (307), she not only likes going "abroad," but finds exposure to public life necessary in order to gather fresh material for her writing (309).

Cavendish's attempt to characterize herself in terms of the early modern world's conceptions of womanhood, to which she feels deeply attached, is nevertheless compromised everywhere by contradiction and hyperbole. Is she a moody, melancholy, contemplative genius, whose delicate modesty and innocence cannot bear the boisterous intrusion of the vulgar world? Or is she an intelligent, talented writer whose gregarious energy and productivity demand both company and fame? Is she a serious artist and thinker, whose overwhelming wealth of ideas requires nurture and expression? Or a foolish, shallow dilettante, inattentive and vain? She tells the reader all of these things, affirming them each with vehement grandiosity, denying them all with unyielding self-doubt. Are her thoughts and ideas really worth writing about? Does the world's opinion matter, or should she disregard it? Should she assert herself, taking responsibility for her desires? She cannot decide.

How does such profound self-division translate itself into action? When Cavendish recounts her failed attempt to save her husband's estate during the Protectorate, she reveals the paralysis that becomes part of her heroic identity. Exiled in Antwerp, she learns that the wives of Royalist owners of sequestered estates could receive allowances. "Necessity"—Cavendish rarely acknowledges acting by choice—forces her to return to England with her brother-in-law, harboring "hopes I should receive a benefit thereby" (296). The reader learns from her account of this episode neither the facts of her case nor the details of her transactions. Instead she emphasizes her lady-like "absolute refusal" either to plead in her own behalf or to plan an effective course of action because "I had a firm faith, or strong opinion, that the pains was more than the gains, and being unpractised in public employments, unlearned in their uncouth ways, ignorant of the humours and dispositions of those persons to whom I was to address my suit, and *not knowing where the power lay,* and being not a good flatterer, *I did not trouble myself or petition my enemies; Besides I am naturally Bashful* . . ." (299–300; emphasis added).

Desperately needing the money, having made the dangerous, painful journey to obtain it, Cavendish then abdicates all responsibility for her property in order to consolidate the performance of female innocence so crucial to her self-conception. Boasting of her ineptitude, she clarifies the way in which female "success" becomes equivalent to male failure, making all action on her part futile. Cavendish's self-defeating representation of her practical abilities stands in vivid contrast to the more constructive approaches taken by several of the other women autobiographers under consideration, all of whom are forced by political exigency to manipulate the constrictions of gender ideology in the effort to save their property.

But Cavendish cannot adjust to emergency; naturally she loses her cause. She ends the account of her failure in an understandable burst of misogynist rage, castigating women who seek "pre-eminence of place" by words: "words rushing against words, thwarting and crossing each other. . . . [I]t is neither words nor place that can advance them, but worth and merit" (299).[18] Cavendish does not connect this wrath against other women's attempts to excel verbally with her own prodigious literary output and acknowledged desire for fame; therefore she misses the opportunity for self-knowledge.[19] It is this failure to merge, to make connections, which pointedly fractures her construction of her identity and her uneven, run-on narrative. Her attempts at coherent structure are repeatedly subverted by her unwillingness to settle on a point or commit herself to an idea. At the beginning of *A True Relation,* for example, she links the unfortunate disruption of her nuclear family with the disastrous disruption of the kingdom; but then the reader learns that she left home out of desire, actively wanting to go to court where, although she describes herself as maladjusted in an attempt to seem meek, she in fact achieves a happy and brilliant marriage.

IV

Insofar as *A True Relation* reveals the urgently problematic, ambivalent nature of female heroism, it can be considered, as scholars have argued, a model of female autobiography. In contrast to Cavendish's equivocal, urgent self-assertion, Ann Fanshawe's autobiography is written as a recollection during her widowhood and is cast in the socially conventional form of the family history. Addressing her *Memoirs* (1676) to her son, she explains that she writes to memorialize her excellent husband for her son's benefit; publication appears never to have been her goal.[20] In Fanshawe's case Mary Mason's argument that women tend to define themselves in relation to others becomes considerably more useful than in the case of the embattled singularity of *A True Relation.* As I hope to show, Fanshawe's text reveals the advantages as well as the price of such self-definition.

Unlike Margaret Cavendish, Ann Fanshawe succeeds remarkably in subsuming contradictions in her representation of her own heroism. The cultural superego through which she defines herself is not the prescribed composite of individualized female character traits with which Cavendish struggles, but rather the seventeenth-century Protestant vision of the perfect wife.[21] Since the British Reformation in the 1530s, the Pauline conception of "holy matrimony," wherein "the husband is head of the wife, even as Christ is head of the Church" (Ephesians 5:23) had been refined and reiterated in Protestant moral, legal, and religious writing. At the very beginning of her narrative, Fanshawe succinctly represents her heroic identity as inhering in her fortunate partnership in such a union, the "great mystery" in which the husband and wife "shall be one flesh," the husband loving the wife as he loves himself, the wife submitting to the husband, reverencing him (Ephesians 5:21–33): "*Glory be to God* we never had but one mind throughout our lives, our souls were wrapped up in each other, our aims and designs one, our loves one, and our resentments one. . . . What ever was real happiness God gave it me in him; but to commend my better half . . . methinks it is to commend myself and so may bear a censure" (103).

At no point in her narrative does Fanshawe deviate from her loyal, loving adherence to this idealized partnership of identical emotions and goals. Indeed she recounts the one moment of matrimonial conflict in her autobiography only in order to reveal the ease with which she overcomes her need for self-assertion. In this isolated instance she discusses her attempt during the height of the Civil War to extract secret information from her husband, Richard, who was performing crucial services for the beleaguered King Charles: "I that was young, innocent, and to that day had never in my mouth 'What news,' begun to think there was more in inquiring into business of public affairs than I thought of" (115). She wheedles and cries, refuses to eat or sleep until he tells her what he knows; he condescends, kisses her, changes the subject, until finally compelled by her weeping and begging to declare that, though his life, fortune, and "every thought" are hers, yet "my honour is my own" (116). It never occurs to Fanshawe to question either openly or deviously an arrangement in which her husband's knowledge is so much freer and more various than her own. Instead the unequal logic of patriarchal power relations is revealed to her through the glow of Richard's undoubted affection and, as she watches him, the scales fall from her eyes: "So great was his reason and goodness, that upon consideration it made my folly appear to me so vile that from that day until the day of his death I never thought fit to ask him any business, but that he communicated freely to me, in order to his estate or family" (116).

The problem for this inquiry becomes, How does a self-defined silent partner manage to represent herself narratively as the hero of her own life? As Fanshawe continually makes clear, her goal is not to act, as a subject, but to be loved, as an object of devotion. The lack of conflict with which she discards her girlish fondness for physical activity in order gladly to assume her dead mother's modest, subdued role as family caretaker indicates the potentially static quality of her life account (110). Yet most of her *Memoirs* tell a lively and engaging story.

Surprisingly, in telling her story, Fanshawe eschews two rhetorical strategies that female autobiographers commonly employ when confronting the contradiction between culturally enjoined silence and the need for self-assertion, or between the peaceful, cyclical orderliness frequently assumed to comprise female destiny and the linear, suspenseful quest narrative characteristic of the representation of male heroism. The first of these strategies, unacknowledged self-assertion, takes the form either of self-idealization disguised as self-deprecation or the overt denial of anger and hostility, prominent emotions that, because they cannot really be ignored, intrude as a subversive subtext. Cavendish, and, as I will show, Alice Thornton, are experts at these double-edged, often self-defeating techniques. At times the violence and self-destructiveness implicit in Fanshawe's unambivalent identification with male superiority are starkly revealed, as in her account of her son Richard's death. "Both my eldest daughters had the smallpox at the same time," she explains, underscoring the virtue of her priorities, "and though I neglected them, and day and night tended my dear son, yet it pleased God they recovered and he died, the grief of which made me miscarry and caused a sickness of 3 weeks" (139). The inhumanity in this passage is shocking precisely because it is exceptional; furthermore, no unacknowledged emotional conflicts surface to disturb the author's untroubled identification with the gendered status quo.

A second narrative strategy that female autobiographers commonly use involves the adoption of a traditionally male quest narrative into the story of the author's romantic adventures, which culminate in her destiny-as-marriage. Anne Halkett uses this strategy with great success, a point to which I will return. Despite her genuine love for her husband and her dramatic location of selfhood in marriage, Fanshawe alone among the four autobiographers under consideration fails to tell the saga of her courtship. For her, the story of self-construction begins, rather than ends, with marriage.

In Fanshawe's case it is clearly the Civil War that liberates her from the acquiescence and passivity required by the gender ideology to which she is profoundly attached; it is therefore the war which gives her story a plot. Because her husband is deeply involved in Royalist intrigue, Fanshawe must frequently act to protect him, along with their joint property interests. Unlike Cavendish, whose ambivalence about acting in the public sphere paralyzes her, Fanshawe responds to the call to independent public action as a challenge. In three daring episodes, for example, she not only makes dangerous, clandestine nightly trips to visit her husband in jail, but also strategizes resourcefully for his freedom (134–35). Imitating romantic tradition, she disguises herself as a man and stands by her husband's side during a shipboard battle with Turkish pirates, inspiring Richard Fanshawe to cry, "Good God, that love can make this change!" (128). She plots and successfully enacts a courageous escape from England, forging her passport in order to join her husband when he is exiled in France (138). Significantly, the perilous exigencies of civil war in no way compel the boldly and publicly active Fanshawe to feel conflict about her female identity. On the contrary, the war simply lends wider meaning to her role as faithful, obedient, and loving wife. Unlike that of Cavendish, her identification with her wifely role is complete and untroubled, enabling her to perform effectively on her husband's behalf. Just as her duty as wife and mother later becomes the rationale for the act of writing her memoirs, so her marriage provides her with a motive and cue for action during the Revolution without requiring her to question prevailing assumptions about gender, which she never does.

For Fanshawe, the difficulty of occupying male heroic space is thus considerably reduced by the Civil War. The external chaos of the Revolution paradoxically releases her from internal conflict by allowing her to merge her private concerns with the larger political environment. Specifically, the exterior strangeness of the political scene enlarges the internal borders of the self, enabling her to act by rendering her vision of the ideal Protestant marriage more expansive and flexible. This point is clarified by the neat division of her narrative into two accounts, one of the Revolution and one of the Restoration. In her retelling of Civil War experiences, Fanshawe structures her representation of marriage with a narrative pattern of death and resurrection, disaster and delivery. Replete with echoes from the Gospels and the Book of Acts, her story of holy matrimony plagued by war becomes a secular scripture recounting separation from and reunion with her husband, who, going about "his master's business" (121), becomes a type of Christ that she can follow, serve, and adore.[22] This scheme works well to propel the narrative forward, but when the two are permanently reunited at the Restoration, the successful pattern inevitably dissolves.

During peacetime, when Richard Fanshawe serves as ambassador to Portugal and Spain, the flamboyant public drama of war, resonant with the depth of emotional life, dwindles to a shallow catalog of ceremonies and gifts that is enlivened only by Ann Fanshawe's sensual love for exotic objects, along with her superb eye for concrete physical detail. Indeed the depiction of her passionate attachment to money and property alters drastically as her experience shifts from war to peace. The pattern of separation from and reunion with her husband, for example, allows her to unite money with love in a blissful epiphany of bourgeois marital goals: "He with all expressions of joy received me in his arms and gave me an hundred pieces of gold, saying, 'I know that thou that keeps my heart so well will keep my fortune.' . . . And now I thought myself a queen, and my husband so glorious a crown that I more valued myself to be call'd by his name than born a princess . . . and his soul doted on me" (115). In peacetime Spain, however, this ecstatic merger of affection and property is reduced to a representation of the once dynamic soldier as a trophy, a colorful, although lifeless, diplomatic artifact: "His suit was trimmed with scarlet taffeta ribbon, his stockings of white silk upon long scarlet silk ones, his shoes black with scarlet shoes' strings and garters, his linen very fine laced with very rich Flanders lace, a black beavour button on the left side, with a jewell of 1200 lb" (164).

Fanshawe's capacity for reverence has given way to the less promising capacity to be dazzled. In the second part of her narrative, her need to be loved is represented in the reiterative rendition of public honors—the banquets, gifts, and canon salutes that celebrate her and her husband by diplomatic requirement (145ff). It is a static picture of power without desire: Fanshawe has become absorbed in the institution, rather than the relationship, of marriage.[23] It is not surprising that her narrative trails off inconclusively after her husband's death, although she survives him by fourteen years.

Ann Fanshawe's memoirs provide an excellent example of the way in which a chaotic period of history involves a woman whose conventionality and single-minded devotion to her husband would otherwise have restricted her to silence and passivity in an engaging and dramatic story. In a wartime irony, her loving adherence to the subject position of wife allows her to play a starring role in the male heroics of action. This paradox collapses when the revolution ends, and to read the memoirs is to become increasingly aware of an inhibited, repressed story. It is not simply that Fanshawe's narration dwindles from war to peace, conflict to stasis, ceasing entirely with the death of her husband and her role as his wife. Rather there is a crucial tale that remains untold, namely, the saga of Fanshawe's female body. During the twenty-two years of her marriage, she gives birth to fourteen children, nine of whom die, and this impressive statistic does not encompass the repeated trauma of miscarriage, including one of triplets. Though during war and peace she is almost constantly pregnant, miscarrying, or giving birth, Fanshawe treats these experiences peripherally, merely mentioning rather than exploring them. This astonishing omission cannot be accounted for by attributing to her an anachronistic reticence about sexuality. It is rather that, in her selection of incidents and her choice of narrative strategies, she assigns a secondary value to those material aspects of her experience that are uniquely female: namely, the capacity to conceive and give birth.

V

Whereas Ann Fanshawe overvalues the male heroics of action to the point of denying the importance of critical aspects of her identity, Alice Thornton makes full use of her female body to construct herself as a hero of endurance. Thornton (1626 / 7–1706 / 7) is an Anglican and Royalist from a distinguished upper-gentry family. Her father, Christopher Wandesford, was Lord Deputy of Ireland. His death forced her mother to return with her family to England during the chaos of the Irish Rebellion in 1641. Thornton's autobiography is a long, bulky account of her childhood, the political upheavals she experienced in Ireland and England, her marriage and numerous pregnancies, her squabbles with relatives, friends, and neighbors, her many illnesses, and her efforts to retain her property.[24]

Upon this variety of selected material Alice Thornton imposes the same narrative pattern that Ann Fanshawe uses to organize the first half of her *Memoirs*: the scriptural sequence of death and resurrection, affliction and delivery. As discussed, Fanshawe creates this structure to convey her love for her husband and to define herself by dramatizing her relationship with him, an imaginative feat made feasible by the intervention of the Civil War in her emotional life. Further, her location of meaning in her relationship with her husband and her idealization of male superiority cause her virtually to ignore her frequent pregnancies and childbearing experiences, to ignore her female body. In contrast, Alice Thornton uses the same narrative pattern precisely to convey her struggles with her body and, in so doing, she seeks to represent herself not as a partner, a secondary ally, but as a hero, a primary object of God's love.

In Thornton's autobiography, her heroic body enacts the trajectory of the questing, surviving, even the competing subject. Delivered from fire (7, 11), revolution (28–32), smallpox (6, 32), drowning (9), and rape (44–47), her body also endures what she represents as the heroism of childbirth. Indeed Thornton's narrative shows itself most vivid and interesting when, for example, she describes in full physical detail the sometimes delightful, often hazardous process of nursing one of her babies (124), the painful phenomenon of a breech birth (95–97), or the grotesque details of the illnesses she suffers as a result of childbirth: "The hair on my head came off, my nails of my fingers and toes came off, my teeth did shake, and ready to come out and grew black" (87–88). In a characteristic passage worth quoting at length, she relates the death of her baby son, providing in the process an intimate and detailed account of the frequent experience of infant mortality in early modern life:

> [A]nd my pretty babe was in good health, sucking his poor mother, to whom my good God had given the blessing of the breast as well as the womb, of that child to whom it was no little satisfaction, while I enjoyed his life; and the joy of it maked me recrute faster, for his sake, that I might do my duty to him as a mother. But it so pleased God to shorten this joy, least I should be too much transported. . . . [F]or on the Friday sennitt after, he began to be very angry and froward. . . . [H]is face when he awaked was full of red round spots like the small pox, being of the compass of a halfpenny, and all whealed white all over. . . . [A]nd, about nine a'clock on Saturday morning he sweetly departed this life, to the great discomfort of his

weak mother, whose only comfort is that the Lord, I hope, has received him . . . [a]nd that my soul may be bettered by all these chas-
tisements He pleaseth to lay upon me, His vile worm and unprof-
itable servant . . . [w]hereby He has corrected me, but not given me
over to death and destruction, for which I humbly magnify His glorious name forever. (124–25)[25]

This passage should help to clarify the ways Thornton embodies her
heroic endurance. But in presenting the components of her claim to
attention as piety, humility, affliction, and rescue, this passage, like
many others in her text, also reveals the extent to which her location of
heroism in her body depends upon pain and loss. Again and again she
falls ill or loses a loved relation, suffering outrageously; yet repeated
sorrows only appear as further "signs of His love to me" (111). Thornton's is the self-sacrificing heroism of the martyr, for whom endurance
is the highest form of activity. In the spiritual pattern to which she ad-
heres, affliction becomes a badge of moral prestige. Disaster and recovery illuminate the identity of the sufferer by marking her as one of
God's chosen, for whom He personally demonstrates both potential
destruction and promised delivery from death. Dame Julian of Nor-
wich "prayed for an illness that would both confirm and deepen her vo-
cation," writes a recent critic, "that illness [was] the gift and sign of her
grace."[26] By choosing the state of prestigious affliction as the projection
of her heroism, Thornton thus adopts an early modern form of piety
that was available to both sexes. More interesting for these purposes,
however, is that, with repetitious intensity, she applies this religious
configuration to her specifically secular, female experiences of marriage and childbirth. As a result her autobiography very clearly drama-
tizes the morality of female self-sacrifice by revealing its spiritual and
psychological dynamics at work in secular life.

Thornton's narrative makes clear that the religious subject position
of prestigious affliction, with its heroic purpose of self-sacrifice meet-
ing a deferred reward, achieves only limited success as a pattern of ad-
justing to reality when transferred to the realm of female secular
experience. I have suggested the ways Thornton's self-conscious identification with her body endows her with heroism and provides a detailed
and revealing account of the monumental physical hardships that a tra-

ditional wife and mother faced and surmounted in seventeenth-century England, all of which lends great conviction to her autobiography. Like that of Cavendish, Thornton's cultural drama centers on issues of female agency: independence, power, and choice. As I argued earlier, Cavendish oscillates wildly between professions of inner weakness and inner strength, often confusing the two and creating as a result a bewildering, run-on narrative structure, in which conflicting claims exist side by side unmediated, demanding equally to be heard. Lacking Cavendish's undisciplined (perhaps aristocratic) arrogance, Thornton also lacks her ambivalence. Consequently she constructs her heroic identity by recognizing that her physical weakness *is* her moral strength and by finding an appropriate form for this paradoxical self-conception in the scriptural sequence of delivery from death.

Despite the greater firmness of her heroic identity, Thornton shares with Cavendish the unresolved problems that beset both female agency and autobiographical writing: the conflict between the emerging value being placed on an individual "self" endowed with singularity and authenticity, and the various antagonisms between this emerging private self and differing cultural idealizations of public values and behavior. Much longer and more consistent than that of Cavendish, Thornton's narrative allows the reader to observe closely the effects of these tensions on the author's construction of a heroics of endurance.

Like the texts of Cavendish and Fanshawe, Thornton's autobiography contains an untold tale, a submerged story which, in Thornton's case, deconstructs many of the meanings she assigns to events. Thornton's characteristic mode of self-presentation involves denying the claims of her ego while simultaneously asserting them in devious boasts couched in the self-sacrificing terms of traditional female virtues. Recounting her mother's generous financial legacy to her, for example, she concludes: "All which I confess far exceeding my merit, but not her entire affection, for my constant being with her in her sorrows and solitudes" (104). Equally typical is her use of illness to compete with siblings, friends, and spouse: if her neighbor falls down the stairs, she falls faster and harder (139); if her husband becomes ill or melancholy, she gets sicker and more depressed (149). Determined to exceed all rivals in illness, accident, misfortune, or pain, Thornton portrays herself as

existing perpetually at death's door, a representation which, if understandable given the actual perils of her life, nevertheless jars oddly with
the fact that she outlives not only her husband, but all nine of her children, lasting until what was for the seventeenth century the remarkably
old age of eighty-one.[27] Anxious to create herself as weak, sick, and
pitiful, Alice Thornton is in fact tough and enduring, a survivor.

Duplicitous humility, petty competition, subversive self-aggran-
dizement turning strength to weakness and weakness to strength: the
disingenuousness that results when these qualities converge in Thornton's subtext is understandable, given the cultural obstacles against female self-assertion. Yet part of the value of her autobiography is the way
it reveals the dangerous implications of the drama of alleged self-sacrifice that characterizes the heroics of endurance. In Thornton's account
of her marriage, anger and aggression are only barely contained by the
counter-mythology of female passivity and innocence that shapes the
primary text.

It is when Thornton gets married—her "great change" as she calls
it—that the Civil War intervenes to play a leading role in determining
her personal destiny. Suddenly the victorious forces of Oliver Crom-
well destroy the peace of her childhood by seizing on her brother's estate, "wherein my father's family was fairly designed for ruin" (61). The
Wandesford family's escape from financial disaster turns out to consist
in offering the fifteen-year-old Alice in marriage, in return for which
the designated groom's uncle promises to retrieve the sequestered
Wandesford property: "Thus the bargain was struck betwixt them before my dear mother and my self ever heard a syllable of this matter"
(61). In other words Thornton's match was an openly loveless deal,
struck for the financial advantage of interested relatives. Although such
economic arrangements were the norm for upper-class marriages
throughout the Middle Ages and the Renaissance, all known evidence
indicates that, by the late seventeenth century, individual choice of a
partner, and as a consequence, companionate marriages, were gaining
in frequency as well as prestige among these classes.[28] Yet, though several of her contemporaries are known to have done so successfully,
Thornton does not contest her fate. It is true that she registers open
anger at the indignity of existing as an object, bartered and compelled:

"Which manner of persuasion to a marriage, with a sword in one hand, and a compliment in another, I did not understand, when a free choice was denied me. Tho' I did not resolve to change my happy estate for a miserable encumbered one in the married; yet I was much afflicted to be threatened against my own inclination (or my future happiness), which I enjoyed under that sweet and dear society and comfort of my most dear parents' conduct" (62). Nevertheless Thornton chooses to submerge her rage at this ruthless disregard for her agency and feelings, piously surrendering her needs to a political and religious configuration of self-sacrifice: "[M]y marriage was laid in the scale to redeem my dear brother's estate from the tyranny of our oppressor, by the sequestration of all that was a friend to loyalty or the Church of God then established in England. But since I was thus disposed, it became my duty to stand my ground in a strange place, and amongst strange people, and that I was resolved to do, by God's grace and divine assistance" (214ff).

This passage concisely delineates an unresolved conflict implicit throughout Alice Thornton's narrative. Does she regard her marriage as chosen or compelled, a tyranny forced upon her or a duty cheerfully and willingly undertaken? Here—and in many other passages where she reminds the reader of the inadequacy of her husband's estate in order to protest that she doesn't care —Thornton represents the sacrifice of her personal happiness as a deed that, if originally compelled by her family, has subsequently become a chosen act of political and domestic altruism, about which she feels both reconciled and proud. But her sense of her own singularity does not in fact consent to be merged so crudely with notions of the collective good, and unsuccessfully repressed anger finds an outlet in the revenge of domestic strife.

This process is clarified in her self-contradictory account of her relationship with her husband. When Alice Thornton eventually becomes a widow, she spares no pains embroidering her sorrow, mourning her late husband as "my chiefest comfort and support" (168), and punctuating her life account with lengthy, grieving odes and pious lamentations. Yet throughout her narrative Thornton portrays her husband as a kindly bumbler, whose melancholia, obstinacy, naïveté, and financial ineptitude reach their apogee in his refusal to listen to her good advice (e.g., 138). In Thornton's portrayal of her husband's weaknesses, she reveals

her peculiar, if unsurprising reaction to the collapse of Royalist male social superiority and political hegemony that so drastically affects the
lives of the women writers under consideration. As I discussed earlier,
Ann Fanshawe, defining herself through relationship, views the social
chaos of the Revolution as an emotional opportunity and makes creative use of disorder by expanding her wifely role as helpmate and companion. In contrast, Alice Thornton, defining herself as a victim of the
males to whose power she has surrendered her fate, can only respond
with rage and a bitter sense of betrayal to their loss of control over their
status and property. Like her father, her brothers, and eventually her
brother-in-law, her husband becomes yet another man who has failed
her. His badly timed death is an additional instance of his desertion
(143); furthermore, his failure to make a will involves her in complicated, exhausting property struggles, extending the consequences of
his fiscal inadequacy well beyond the grave and providing posthumous
material for her anger and disgust (e.g., 181–83).

Undeterred by the magnitude of her own revelations, Thornton insists on describing her awful marriage to the incredulous reader as that
of "a dear and loving couple" (175, 176). It is not that, like Cavendish,
she bewilders us with the complexity of her feelings. Her contempt for
her husband is dominating, consistent, and whole. It is rather that, in refusing to acknowledge her obvious rage at being forced to marry a man
she does not respect, she never attempts to reconcile her anger with the
cultural demand that she be a loving and devoted wife. This inability, or
unwillingness, to consciously acknowledge the roots of her own suffering constitutes a refusal, even perhaps an evasion, of self-knowledge.
Therefore unfortunate history repeats itself.

In an uncanny instance of the oppressed become oppressor, Thornton arranges the marriage of her fourteen-year-old daughter to a much
older man with the same economic pragmatism and thoughtless domination that determined the identical fate she had confronted with re-
luctance and sorrow. But she displays neither memory of her own unhappiness nor awareness that she is bartering her daughter's destiny. In
recounting her motives for arranging the match, she cites economics
and—what else?—illness: "My own great illness, and many weakness
on myself . . . did press much upon my spirit, lest we both should be

snatched from our dear children, and they left in a forlorn condition of both their parents gone" (154). In other words, Thornton presents her carefully and explicitly calculated decision to marry off her daughter not as a chosen act for which she is responsible, but—to quote Carol Gilligan's study of female moral and psychological development—"as an act of sacrifice, a submission to necessity where the absence of choice precludes responsibility." Furthermore, the reader learns that Thornton rushes this marriage, which is greatly disapproved of by her relatives, in order to quash scandalous rumors that she herself is romantically involved with her daughter's fiancé (229). But Thornton expresses no doubts that she has behaved with the most scrupulous maternal benevolence since "God is on my side" (230). The dubious logic inherent in such an unacknowledged assertion of personal power comprises an evasion of responsibility that is "critical to maintaining the innocence [the woman] considers necessary for self-respect," although it "contradicts the reality of her participation in the . . . decision."[29]

VI

Like Cavendish, Fanshawe, and Thornton, Anne Halkett (1623–99) is an upper-class Anglican and Royalist who struggles to define herself within a culturally prescribed conception of femaleness while, at the same time, her social and personal horizons are being drastically altered by the Civil War. Among the four autobiographical texts considered here, Halkett's memoirs (1677–78) display the firmest grasp of the emerging cultural narrative of identity that privileges a coherent, unified self. While the differences that distinguish her text are those of degree rather than kind, exploring the contrasts illuminates ways in which subtle variations in psyche and circumstance can converge to affect the construction of female heroism.[30]

The first significant difference in Halkett's text is her depiction of her relationship with her mother. Among the four autobiographers discussed here, Halkett alone refrains from idealizing her mother. All four writers recognize the significance of the mother-daughter bond in the formation of their heroic identities. Cavendish presents her adored mother as the perfect embodiment of the Renaissance cultural ideal of the feminine; Ann Fanshawe makes her claim to attention as the special object of her mother's love, gladly subduing her more active personality traits in order to assume with unbroken continuity her dead mother's passive domestic role; and Alice Thornton, angry with almost everyone else in her life, reserves a special respect and tenderness for her mother. In contrast, Anne Halkett's story and her heroism begin with conflict between her widowed mother and herself. "In the year 1644 I confess I was guilty of an act of disobedience," she tells the reader (11), and with this declaration, her narrative begins.

Halkett's youthful disobedience involves a clandestine engagement to Thomas Howard, eldest son of Edward, Lord Howard of Escrick. As she relates it, this romance was explicitly forbidden by her mother, both for economic reasons and also, Halkett suggests, from sheer intransigence on her mother's part (14). The drama of this episode unfolds as a counterpoint between Halkett's audacious romantic stratagems and secret encounters with Howard and her struggles with her "offended mother, who nothing could pacify" (15). Telling Howard she will never marry him without parental consent while telling her family she will never break her engagement unless Howard marries another, she never explicitly admits to defying her mother's authority, although her actions clearly reveal that she remains unterrified by parental power. The battle of wills that ensues between mother and daughter takes revealing shape in the following dialogue: "I said I could not but regret what ever had occasioned her displeasure . . . but I was guilty of no unhandsome action to make me ashamed; and therefore, what ever were my present misfortune, I was confident to evidence before I died that no child she had had greater love and respect to her, or more obedience. . . . To which she replied, 'It seems you have a good opinion of yourself' (17)." Thus Halkett's independence and self-respect are interpreted by her mother as willfulness and conceit.

Although she refuses to capitulate to parental tyranny, Halkett nevertheless suffers painfully from her mother's disapproval. After Howard's father finally sends him to France to "secure" him from Halkett, Halkett's mother declines to speak to her daughter (except to reproach her) for fourteen months, commenting "with much bitterness she did hate to see me. That word I confess struck deeply to my heart" (20). When Howard eventually proves faithless, returning to England to marry an heiress, Halkett makes a rapid recovery, in which "nothing troubled me more then my mother's laughing at me" (22). Faced with humiliation, defeat, and the double rejection of mother and lover, Halkett's response is characteristic: rather than patiently enduring her grief, she struggles hard against it, finally outwitting her mother by asking a relative to find her a place in a Dutch nunnery for Protestants. The sympathetic relation then persuades Halkett's mother to forgive her daughter, "and from that time she received me again to her favor, and ever after used me more like a friend then a child" (20).

This last point reveals Halkett's romance with Howard as not only a spirited young woman's search for passionate adventure, but also as a struggle for freedom and equality. That she would choose to undertake, rather than to deny, ignore, or submerge this conflict with authority distinguishes Halkett from Cavendish, Fanshawe, and Thornton. As her conduct and resolution of the struggle imply, Halkett confronts, even instigates conflict, using it as a means of attaining independence. After Halkett wins recognition as an adult from her mother, that authority figure disappears from her autobiographical tale; even her mother's death is never reported. Halkett lays claim to her life story as her own.

Halkett's early conflict with her mother assumes importance as a revelation of her singular personality and character; it also provides a basis for understanding her construction of a heroic identity. As many scholars have argued, the successful creation of the modern ideal of the coherent self often requires painful separation from origins and subsequent acts of conquest, both characteristically masculine achievements. Leaving aside the issue of the desirability of this idea (why does identity need to be achieved through separation from the mother and dominance?), these are the characteristics of the oedipal plot.[31] In literature this mode of male heroism often takes narrative form as a linear quest, in which the hero struggles to achieve his destiny. The conception of heroic destiny as achieved through the active surmounting of conflict runs counter to a common cultural expectation that women's lives will assume a unified, cyclical form in accordance with unbroken, recurring traditions. As Halkett's conflict with her mother makes clear, independence for a woman is often achieved at the expense of love and approval.

One important exception enables female heroes to represent themselves without punishment in the active, linear form usually preserved
for men: that is, when marriage is construed as the destiny that the female hero struggles through romantic conflict to achieve.[32] With its
origins in religious and romantic story, this structure of course reaches
its primary secular expression in the novel. It is Halkett's confident
grasp of this narrative strategy, which she uses to represent herself as a
hero actively creating—rather than avoiding (Cavendish), adapting (Fanshawe), or enduring (Thornton)—her unique destiny, that distinguishes
her narrative from those of the other women considered here. Unlike
Cavendish, she directly acknowledges her needs; unlike Thornton, she
eschews the heroics of endurance; unlike Fanshawe, she recognizes
that, with the achievement of a peacetime marriage, her active heroism
ends.

Halkett's penchant for conflict-engendering romance and her narrative skill combine with the Civil War to give scope to the creation of
her heroism. This convergence can best be perceived in her account of
her long, ambiguous connection with Colonel Joseph Bampfield (designated throughout her text as "C. B."), which comprises the bulk of the
narrative. C. B. is a dashing, handsome cad, a nonfictional predecessor
of Jane Austen's Willoughby and Wickham, whom Halkett comes to
know as a friend of her brother's. This exciting, adventurous soldier op-
erates at the center of Royalist intrigue, and he and Halkett together en-
gineer the daring, theatrical escape of the Duke of York from England,
an episode Halkett relates in full dramatic detail (23–26). In the highly
charged atmosphere of the Revolution, love and politics inevitably
unite. Although C. B. is married when Halkett meets him, he convinces
her that he has had news of his wife's death, and the two become se-
cretly engaged.

Is C. B.'s wife dead or not? It seems astonishing, even impossible that
Halkett would not be able to determine this simple fact, yet, whatever
measure of self-deception may have influenced her discernment, her
account of the sheer difficulty of obtaining reliable information during
the chaos of the war, particularly when one is on the losing side, makes
the obstacles to her knowing the truth entirely credible. Forced to leave

London and hide in the north after the Duke of York's escape, Halkett is separated from C. B. and subjected to numerous conflicting accounts about his integrity. Relatives appear from distant parts of England, swearing his wife is alive and well; equally believable witnesses come forth to persuade her that he is indeed a widower. She receives ominous letters from disapproving siblings, one of whom challenges C. B. to a duel, where C. B. vows when wounded that he believes his wife is dead and that he is eternally devoted to Anne Murray (later Halkett). Various reunions with her clandestine lover alternately reassure and torment her, and the reader enters sympathetically into her powerfully rendered wavering and frustration. Halkett's skill at involving the reader in the suspense surrounding C. B.'s personal life not only draws the narrative forward; the story of one woman's wartime romance also gradually expands in significance to encompass the larger theme of the impossibility of knowing. In this late seventeenth-century saga of political intrigue and social disorder, the reliability of communications can finally be determined only by inner resolution. Despite recurring doubts, Halkett keeps her faith in C. B.'s loyalty until James Halkett comes along and convinces her that C. B.'s wife is still alive. That she believes James Halkett, whose information she has no more apparent reason to trust than anyone else's, simply means that she has overcome her conflict and achieved her destiny by finding her future husband.

Another way to say this is that Anne Halkett constructs her heroism according to the demands of what she conceives as a separate, inner self. The amount of courage required for a single woman thus to view herself and act independently is clarified in the extent to which she both risks and successfully avoids ruinous social scandal. The episode that best makes this point is her account of her virtual expulsion from Naworth Castle, where, having sought a purportedly secure hiding place with Charles and Anne Howard after her dangerous rescue of the Duke of York, she finds herself vulnerable to the sexual slander of a duplicitous minister, a Tartuffe in whom she unfortunately confides the details of her relationship with C. B. Although Halkett fully acknowledges her vulnerability as a woman alone, involved in a questionable engagement and supported by neither wealth nor consistent family loyalty, she never represents herself as a victim, a misunderstood and mistreated case of injured virtue. Instead she takes full moral and social responsibility for her actions and desires.[33] For example, although recognizing the dangerous instability of her clandestine relationship with C. B., she nevertheless refrains from blaming his faithlessness for her plight. Although she acknowledges what she construes as an appropriate distinction between the needs of public and private life, she does so without bitterness, refusing to dwell on it as the major issue determining her conduct. Instead she assesses the difficult attachment forthrightly as her own choice, made according to her individual desire:

> I know I may be condemned as one that was too easily prevailed with, but this I must desire to be considered: he was one who I had been conversant with for several years before; one that professed a great friendship to my beloved brother Will; he was unquestionably loyal [i.e., politically], handsome, a good scholar . . . at least he made it appear such to me, and whatever misfortune he brought upon me I will do him that right as to acknowledge I learnt from him many excellent lessons of piety and virtue and to abhor and detest all kind of vice. . . . From the prejudice which that opinion brought upon me I shall advise all never to think a good intention can justify what may be scandalous. . . . And I confess I did justly suffer the scourge of the tongue for exposing my self upon any consideration to what might make me liable to it, for which I condemn myself as much as my severest enemy (28).

Although Halkett does manage to find essential protectors after leaving Naworth Castle, her text is also full of instances in which she acts effectively alone, not only in behalf of her property (79ff) or her reputation (53–54), but also altruistically: for example, when she nurses wounded soldiers with such skill and tenacity that her performance is rewarded by Charles II (55–56). As in her remarks about scandal (just quoted), Halkett demonstrates in all of these actions her respect for the social and political culture that, in her erotic life, she has defied. Her triumph as a determined female is to recognize the emerging social distinction between public and private life and never to allow herself to become marginal. Paradoxically, such a determination means the end of her heroism: her narrative breaks off abruptly in 1656, the year of her marriage.[34]

VII

With the partial exception of the religious narrative, female self-assertion in late seventeenth-century England was regarded as neither moral nor suitable: Aphra Behn was considered a scandal; Anne Finch lived in bitter seclusion; Margaret Cavendish was laughed at as an exhibitionist and a fool. Despite this virtually unchallenged injunction to female reticence, a number of women made important contributions to the early development of English secular autobiography, in which they create themselves as heroes of their own lives. The women discussed here do not write in a prevailing spirit of challenge or defiance. Rather they identify themselves as well-established, often conservative voices within the mainstream culture: they are traditional wives and mothers of the Anglican upper classes, actively loyal to husband, country, and king.

Viewed from a historical perspective, the traditionalism of these women—their attachment to established patriarchal values and goals—can be seen to have played a paradoxical role in freeing them to write. All four women are Royalists, confronting temporary social and political defeat in the English Civil War; and their active participation in wartime events suggests the way that social chaos, upsetting the conventional gender arrangements to which all four women adhere, can generate female heroism.[35] While all four autobiographers witness the loss of social superiority and political hegemony of the men who dominate their world, their consequent attempts to rectify and compensate for this loss of status, money, and power give their lives an added public dimension that drastically alters their horizons. Indeed they discover that the only way for a female effectively and openly to defend the status quo is to break its rules, by violating the culturally prescribed definition of women as modest, passive, silent, and obedient.

In their autobiographical responses to this quandary of conflicting demands, all four women under consideration share certain narrative and behavior patterns that, as scholars of women's literature have been pointing out, can be identified as culturally female. Like Elizabeth I, they extricate themselves from potential defeat and survive. With the exception of Fanshawe, however, their narratives do not focus on survival, but on their struggles to maintain it. The intersection of the female with problematic agency, or agency beset by contradictions and compromise, describes the mode of heroism that comes to dominate English literature in the later seventeenth century.

"Vigorous most / When most unactive deem'd":
Gender and the Heroics of Endurance in Milton's
Samson Agonistes, Aphra Behn's *Oroonoko,* and
Mary Astell's *Some Reflections upon Marriage*

I

The late seventeenth century in England is often called the age of the failed epic. As its traditionally defined task, the epic celebrates the civilizing components of military conquest. Perhaps not surprisingly, epic idealizations did not convince a culture in which all power relations involving hierarchy and subjection were being eagerly scrutinized and violently redesigned. Indeed, literary representations of the heroic in the Restoration indicate that the experience of Civil War and its aftermath robbed "slaughter and gigantic deeds" (*Paradise Lost* 11.659) of much of their charisma.[1] Traditional forms of male heroics—concerned with movement and adventure, rescue, exploration, and conquest—characteristically survive in overblown, grandiose representations, as in the heroic drama; or parody, as in *Hudibras.*[2] The most famous epic poem of the period, *Paradise Lost,* decides that marriage is the truly significant human endeavor and wages a full-scale attack on military glory as flashy, anachronistic, and trivial:

> Since first this Subject for Heroic Song
> Pleas'd me long choosing, and beginning late;
> Not sedulous by Nature to indite
> Wars, hitherto the only Argument
> Heroic deem'd, chief maistry to dissect
> With long and tedious havoc fabl'd Knights
> In Battles feign'd; the better fortitude

Of Patience and Heroic Martyrdom
Unsung; or to describe Races and Games,
Or tilting Furniture, emblazon'd Shields,
Impreses quaint, Caparisons and Steeds;
Bases and tinsel Trappings, gorgeous Knights
At Joust and Tournament; then marshall'd Feast
Serv'd up in Hall with Sewers, and Seneschals;
The skill of Artifice or Office mean,
Not that which justly gives Heroic name
To Person or to Poem. Mee of these
Nor skill'd nor studious, higher Argument
Remains.

                                        (9.25–43)

In this passage Milton does not simply attack the phallic heroics of action; he also announces his intention radically to transform its traditional idealizations of violent conquest. He proposes an alternative and, he argues, superior dimension of heroic identity: that which privileges not the active confrontation with danger, but the capacity to suffer calamity and disaster with patience and fortitude. As Milton's representations of epic heroism make clear, by the late seventeenth century, the heroics of endurance, gendered normatively as female, had achieved sufficient prestige to become the primary model of literary heroism. To elaborate this argument, I will examine three Restoration texts: Milton's *Samson Agonistes* (1671), Aphra Behn's *Oroonoko* (1688), and Mary Astell's *Some Reflections upon Marriage* (1700). When viewed together, these texts reveal a self-conscious effort to revalue and transform the male heroics of action. From Milton's text to Astell's, the construction and performance of the heroic are accomplished increasingly in terms that are, if ambiguously, nevertheless predominantly, gendered female. All three texts deconstruct the phallic heroics of action by presenting a sustained critique of physical strength as the source of male privilege; and all three texts focus on compromised agency, or agency inscribed in contradictions, as the defining condition of the heroic. This condition is represented first in the hero's position of being seduced into slavery and second in the relation of the hero's slavery to marriage.

II

In *Samson Agonistes,* the hero first appears as a blind slave, a condition that defines him throughout the play, demanding interpretation. Scholars have defined slavery in terms of power and property relations, variously exploring the slave's alienation and domination. Recently, Orlando Patterson has argued that "archetypically slavery was a substitute for death in war." Emphasizing the ways in which a dishonored acquiescence in physical powerlessness was all that stood between the slave and death, Patterson demonstrates how that violence disenfranchised slaves from the symbolic economy of the culture as well: "Slaves differed from other human beings in that they were not allowed freely to integrate the experience of their ancestors into their lives, to inform their understanding of social reality with the inherited meanings of their natural forebears, or to anchor the living present in any conscious community of memory."[3] I will return to the particular ways the texts I am considering use the condition of slavery to interpret violence and death. Here I would like to stress that, when we are first introduced to Samson, his slavery makes manifest his alienation from his own past. Indeed, that the hero is bereft of a usable past, a "community of memory," becomes an informing structural principle of the play.

As Mary Ann Radzinowicz has shown, in a bold revision of the Judges narrative, Milton begins his play where earlier tragedies, such as those by Shakespeare and Marlowe, end: that is, with the defeated hero. Whereas in *Dr. Faustus* and *Macbeth* we witness the entirety of the hero's courageous if doomed trajectory, in *Samson Agonistes* the hero's exploits have become a remembrance of things past, recited, rather than enacted, as a choral lament.[4] At the beginning of the play, the Chorus encounters Samson paralyzed, "dead more than half," and trying to reconcile his divine genealogy and fabled exploits with the horror of his present life. Appalled at the concrete, physical spectacle of fallen might (soiled clothes, drooping head, foul odor, blank eyes), the Chorus exclaims,

> O change beyond report, thought, or belief!
> See how he lies at random, carelessly diffus'd,

> With languish't head unpropt,
> As one past hope, abandon'd,
> And by himself given over;
> In slavish habit, ill-fitted weeds
> O'er worn and soil'd;
> Or do my eyes misrepresent? Can this be hee,
> That Heroic, that Renown'd,
> Irresistible *Samson*? whom unarm'd
> No strength of man, or fiercest wild beast could withstand;
> Who tore the Lion, as the Lion tears the Kid,
> Ran on embattled Armies clad in Iron,
> And weaponless himself,
> Made Arms ridiculous
>
> . . . .
> Which shall I first bewail,
> Thy Bondage or lost Sight,
> Prison within Prison
> Inseparably dark?
> Thou art become (O worst imprisonment!)
> The Dungeon of thyself.
>
> (117–31, 151–56)

To the Chorus Samson is fallen, his legendary career over. As the passage just quoted makes clear, this conviction comes from a concrete conception of Samson's heroic identity as grounded in his physical strength and warlike victories over his enemies: a traditional phallic heroics of action. Yet, as he makes clear in the invocation to book 9 of *Paradise Lost,* Milton, concerned with a "better fortitude," finds this conception of the heroic inadequate and deluded.[5] In Samson's long opening soliloquy, recited before the Chorus enters the scene, the hero does not so much lament the loss of his strength as interrogate its meaning, asking,

> But what is strength without a double share
> Of wisdom? Vast, unwieldly, burdensome,
> Proudly secure, yet liable to fall
> By weakest subtleties, not made to rule,
> But to subserve where wisdom bears command.

God, when he gave me strength, to show withal
How slight the gift was, hung it in my Hair.
                                (53—59)[6]

Far from elegiacally recalling his past exploits, Samson in fact rejects his past, finding it unusable: "to mee strength is my bane" (63). Indeed the text is ambiguous at several points about whether or not Samson still possesses his fabulous physical might (173—74, 586—87); clearly this manifestation of his legendary heroism is no weapon against present misery. As the opening soliloquy indicates, Samson's heroic career has entered a new phase, a reflective phase that interests Milton much more than the performance of amazing feats. Paralyzed, Samson himself revalues his past by ruminating upon his present compromised agency. Is he the betrayer of his own mission or helplessly abandoned by God; self-enslaving or seduced into slavery; actor or acted upon; male or female?

As I have tried to show throughout this study, critical analysis reveals the complex ways in which normatively defined gendered positions break down in the Renaissance, both from self-generated discursive contradictions and from the empirical evidence of historical experience. Nevertheless these prescriptive norms remain operative and, as such, become informing principles in representations of gender relations and heroism. Given the ubiquitous deployment of these norms throughout Renaissance texts, Samson as hero in Milton's play clearly inhabits a subject position gendered female. It is not simply that Samson bitterly taunts himself as effeminate. As slave to the Philistines, he also occupies the passive position of object of the hostile gaze, subject to his enemies' mocking scrutiny and literally rendered helpless by blindness to return the predatory look: "Betray'd, Captiv'd, and both my Eyes put out, / Made of my Enemies the scorn and gaze" (33—34). Second, he explicitly conflates his present slavery with his former position as husband: "Foul effeminacy held me yok't / Her Bond-slave" (410—11). By thus inscribing himself within a burgeoning seventeenth-century critique of marriage that equated wifehood with slavery, Samson by implication defines himself as a wife.[7] Further, Samson's gifts from God bind him to silence, inscribed in Renaissance discourses as a female virtue.

Whereas men characteristically are found wanting in terms of insufficient eloquence, Samson's crime is "shameful garrulity" (491), one of the most frequently denounced female transgressions.

But what does it mean when the "strongest of mortal men" (168), the phallic hero par excellence, occupies a female position, one that, like the Chorus, we tend to regard negatively as vulnerable, passive, and subjected—all Renaissance meanings of the word "effeminate"?[8] I argue that, rather than representing the loss of his heroic identity, Samson's slavery and passivity are constituent of it. Thus the gendered shifts in Samson's identity do not simply signify a descent from former greatness; the deconstruction of his hypermasculinity instead represents a shift in the mode of conceptualizing heroic experience itself.

The components of this shift, and its painfulness, become apparent in the despairing exchange between Samson and his father, Manoa. Upon first entering the scene, the father does not recognize his son (331–36). Manoa's subsequent shocked lament about Samson's condition reveals that his view of his son's heroic identity resembles that of the Chorus: that is, he evaluates Samson's worth according to his effectiveness as a hero of action:

> O miserable change! is this the man,
> That invincible *Samson,* far renown'd,
> The dread of *Israel's* foes, who with a strength
> Equivalent to Angels' walk'd thir streets,
> None offering fight; who single combatant
> Duell'd thir Armies rank't in proud array,
> Himself an Army.
>   (340–46)

The ensuing miscommunication between father and son is awful; it takes shape as conflicting interpretations of and allegiances to the hero's past. Upon perceiving his son's blindness and despondency, Manoa loudly bewails his betrayed fatherhood, blaming God. In reply, Samson tries desperately to dwell on his disastrous marriage, emphasizing in no uncertain terms what is important to him. But Manoa denies his son's view of the source of his own misery, dismissively uttering one of the less memorable Miltonic lines, "I cannot praise thy marriage choices,

Son" (420). The father thus willfully misses the significance of his son's plight, implicitly defining as trivial Samson's preoccupation with his marriage and emphasizing instead Samson's failure as destroyer of the Philistines and liberator of the Israelites.

At this point the Chorus colludes with Manoa's insistent erasures of Samson's past. Until Dalila physically enters the scene, forcing a confrontation, the Chorus refuses either to comprehend or even to acknowledge the significance of Samson's marriage. When, with bitter sorrow, the hero angrily recounts his virtual castration at the hands of his wife (530–40), demanding a response, the Chorus anxiously offers, "Desire of wine and all delicious drinks, / Which many a famous Warrior overturns, / Thou couldst repress" (541–43). But Samson's sufferings are not about alcoholism. He desperately replies, "But what avail'd this temperance, not complete / Against another object more enticing?" (558–59). Now Manoa interjects. Vowing to ransom Samson, he expresses hope in the shape of a wild fantasy of the return of his son's former heroic style.[9] Ignored, Samson realizes that returning to his father's house will turn him into a kind of useless wife, sitting "idle on the household hearth, / A burdenous drone; to visitants a gaze, / Or pitied object" (566–68). Thus the exchange between Manoa and Samson creates the most agonized moment of loss in the play, concluding with Samson wishing for death (594–98) and the Chorus vehemently protesting the injustices of God (668–704).

Manoa and the Chorus are not simply repressed and oblivious; they are also anachronistic in their conception of heroism. As Samson tries repeatedly to tell them, the arena of significance—the arena in which he has endeavored and failed—is not military conquest, but marriage. As is often pointed out, one of the major revisions of Judges in the play is Milton's decision to have Samson and Dalila be married. Indeed, Joseph Wittreich has shown that all of Milton's alterations of the source material amount to an intensification of concern with marriage and deliverance.[10]

Milton's representation of marriage as heroic in the play (as well as in the divorce tracts and in *Paradise Lost*) continues, and perhaps sums up, a century of Protestant commentary in which the public dignity and cosmic significance of marriage are vehemently asserted. As many scholars have shown, during and after the Reformation and coinciding with the centralization of the nation-state, English Protestants developed both political and religious discourses that compared the organization and structure of authority in the family to that of the church and the state.[11] Rather than distinguishing sharply between personal and public concerns and subordinating the former to the latter, this discourse attempts to equate spiritual, public, and private realms by analogizing the husband to God and the king, the wife to the church and the kingdom. As Carole Pateman sums up, "During the political ferment of the seventeenth century . . . conjugal relations and the marriage contract were as central to political debate as the relation between king and subject and the social contract. The terms . . . of the two contracts were used to argue about the proper form of marriage and political rule."[12]

The analogy between the state and the family is, of course, an ancient invention rather than an English Protestant one; but in Renaissance England the Protestants dramatized it with newly elaborated detail and intensity. Arising in part as an attempt to overthrow the prestige of celibacy, Protestant sexual discourse proliferated in a large quantity of widely publicized sermons and tracts idealizing "holy matrimony" as the most critical endeavor of a person's entire spiritual, personal, and public life. Whether the Protestants stress the obstacles or the rewards inherent in marriage, the crucial point becomes their consensus that this relationship constitutes the arena in which the individual can struggle and meet death or defeat, triumph or salvation. To quote Alexander Niccholes, writing in 1615, for example, "Marriage is an adventure, for whosoever marries, adventures; he adventures his peace, his freedom, his liberty, his body; yea, and sometimes his soul too." Furthermore, undertaking this quest, "the means either to exalt on high to preferment, or cast down headlong to destruction," becomes "this one and absolutely greatest action of a man's whole life," requiring the unwavering commitment characteristic of the hero and assuming the properties of inevitable destiny: "as thereon depending the future good or evil of a man's whole after-time and days." Marriage is a perilous odyssey, a voyage on a dangerous sea, "wherein so many shipwreck for want of better knowledge and advice upon a rock."[13]

Unlike earlier, doctrinal commentary on the subject, Protestant discourse dwells upon the heroic marriage as a lived relationship. As I have argued at length elsewhere, this detailed focus on sexual and domestic behavior tends to analogize public and private life and to grant them equal importance. Almost as an unacknowledged corollary, the discourse of companionate marriage moves toward a conception of mutuality between husband and wife, thus bringing to light potential contradictions that challenge the principles of hierarchy and subordination characterizing the distribution of authority in patriarchal marriage.[14] Thus such issues as whether or not a couple needs parental consent in order to marry, or the precise nature and extent of wifely obedience (to name two problems besetting Samson's marriages) become particularly vexed.

Discussions of individual choice of a spouse and the often contradictory need for parental consent in marriage present compelling examples of the double-mindedness of heroic marital discourse. In 1624 the Jacobean Vicar of Banbury, William Whately, declares not atypically that a couple need not obey their parents—"in not suffering them to marrie in the Lord, but offering to force them marrie against the will of God"—only to declare shortly thereafter that a couple marrying without parental consent lives in sin until "they have procured an after-consent, to ratify that which ought not to have been done before the consent."[15] Similarly, wifely obedience is lionized ("By nature woman was made man's subject"),[16] while at the same time material is provided for its subversion: women should never obey husbands who urge them to do "what is forbidden by God."[17] Furthermore, while wives' subjection is absolute (rising against husbands is the equivalent of rising against God), some writers encourage women not only to disobey, but actively to seek to correct erring husbands.[18] And subjection that is conceived as absolute and natural is nevertheless defined as merely temporal, temporary: "Her place is indeed a place of inferiority and subjection, yet the nearest to equality that may be."[19]

However one assesses heroism and delegates moral responsibility in *Samson Agonistes,* I wish to emphasize the ways these issues are dramatized in the conflicted terms of heroic marital discourse. Linking the public and private spheres, Samson himself justifies his marriages in terms of his divine assignment:

> The first I saw at *Timna,* and she pleas'd
> Mee, not my Parents, that I sought to wed,
> The daughter of an Infidel: they knew not
> That what I motion'd was of God; I knew
> From intimate impulse, and therefore urg'd
> The Marriage on.
>
> (219–24)

Notably, the doubts and ambiguities surrounding Samson's marriages are here couched in the problematic terms of the need for parental consent. Further, Samson and Dalila become embroiled in disputes about the boundaries between the public and private spheres and about wifely obedience and subordination. Dalila first attempts to seduce the blinded Samson with declarations of her love and promises of domestic security, possibilities that she ironically presents both as subversive of his public life and as imprisoning (e.g., 790–818). When Samson responds with rage, she next asserts loyalty to her people as a reason for betraying her husband. Interestingly, Dalila manipulates the ambiguities in the rhetoric of wifely subordination, hinting that to obey Samson would be to do "what is forbidden by God": "It would be to ensnare an irreligious / Dishonorer of *Dagon*: what had I / To oppose against such powerful arguments?" (860–62). Samson protests with an absolutist definition of wifely obedience, eliding the ambiguities that in fact characterize that concept. He replies that, according to the rules of marriage, *he* has become her country, her world: "Being once a wife, for me thou wast to leave / Parents and country" (885–86). Rebuffed, Dalila proudly avenges and defends herself in similarly absolutist terms as a celebrated woman "who to save / Her country from a fierce destroyer, chose / Above the faith of wedlock bands" (984–86).

In constructing her argument, Dalila speciously subordinates the private to the public sphere ("To the public good / Private respects must yield" [867–68]). From Samson's point of view and, indeed, from the construction of the play, Dalila's final outrage is to claim a space for herself in the public sphere. Yet Samson also diminishes the importance of the private sphere, which, as we have seen, is distinguished in heroic marital discourse as having equal significance with the public, to which it is analogously yoked. Evading the complex terms of the heroic marriage upon which he had previously relied ("I was no private," he insists with contempt, "but a person rais'd / With strength sufficient and command from Heav'n / To free my Country" [1211–13]), Samson ignores his own (and the play's) insistent knowledge of the central significance of his marriages to his heroism and identity.[20]

In their antagonistic manipulations of Protestant marital discourse, Samson and Dalila both fall prey to the contradictions that are already embedded in its terms. With the logical inconsistency of self-interest, each attempts to purify and simplify what is muddy and complex. Indignant and confused, the Chorus responds to Samson and Dalila's wrathful marital encounter with a fierce, frustrated assertion of absolute male superiority:

> But virtue which breaks through all opposition,
> And all temptation can remove,
> Most shines and most is acceptable above.
> Therefore God's universal Law
> Gave to the man despotic power
> Over his female in due awe,
> Nor from that right to part an hour,
> Smile she or lour:
> So shall he least confusion draw
> On his whole life, not sway'd
> By female usurpation, nor dismay'd.
>   (1050–60)

In its lack of logic, this passage recalls Thomas Hobbes's assertion that the only reason for a husband's superiority in marriage is that no one can obey two masters: in short, there is no natural reason. If marital politics were to follow nature, the power and knowledge of mothers would allow them to retain their (naturally) superior position.[21] Closer perhaps to Milton is John Locke's recognition that a husband and wife, "though they have but one common concern, yet having different understandings, will unavoidably sometimes have different wills too; it therefore being necessary that the last determination—i.e., the rule— should be placed somewhere, it naturally falls to the man's share, *as the abler and the stronger*" (emphasis added).²² Locke unambiguously cites superior physical strength as the natural basis of male privilege; but, as we have seen, physical strength is precisely the heroic quality that *Samson Agonistes* deconstructs, subjecting its meaningfulness to angry and bewildered scrutiny.

Interestingly, in Protestant discourse, the necessary virtue required of the marital hero of either sex is not physical strength, but patience.²³ After witnessing Samson's encounter with the Philistine blowhard, Harapha, whose cowardly bullying exposes traditional phallic heroics as no more than parody, the Chorus finally realizes that a new mode of heroism is called for. Dismissing "the brute and boist'rous force of violent men / Hardy and industrious to support / Tyrannic power" (1273–75), Samson's contemporaries announce that

> Patience is more oft the exercise
> Of Saints, the trial of thir fortitude,
> Making them each his own Deliverer,
> And Victor over all
> That tyranny or fortune can inflict,
> Either of these is in thy lot,
> *Samson,* with might endu'd
> Above the Sons of men; but sight bereav'd
> May chance to number thee with those
> Whom patience finally must crown.
>   (1287–96)

Patience in the face of inevitable affliction; the moral prestige such affliction grants the sufferer, who is personally chosen by God to endure; obedience, humility, fortitude: the qualities privileged in the heroics of endurance are the same as those used to construct the Renaissance idealization of woman. These parallels would at first seem odd in a text so framed by, and embedded in, masculine constructs as *Samson Agonistes* is. As Michael Lieb points out, despite the Chorus's idealization of Samson as a patient sufferer, he is no saint: "The outcome of his *agon* with Harapha is one that moves him to an ultimate act of glorious and triumphant violence."²⁴ Second, however problematic traditional male heroics turn out to be, Manoa delivers a ringing endorsement of Samson's death by praising his legendary exploits. In my reading of the play, Manoa's tautological view ("nothing but well and fair" and "*Samson* hath quit himself / Like *Samson,* and heroicly hath finish'd / A life Heroic" [1723, 1709−11]) presents a denial and revision of reality; but the father's eloquence at least renders ambiguous the nature of the son's heroic identity by insisting on the need for interpretation. Several other factors also would seem to cast doubt on granting a positive valence to the female in this play. I refer to the rampant misogyny that inscribes Dalila and characterizes many of the choral mutterings (e.g., 710−24), as well as the curious fact that Milton excises Samson's mother, who plays such a critical part in Judges, a rather drastic revision of the source.[25] Further, in "The Argument," Milton suppresses mention of Samson's encounter with Dalila, which is arguably the central event of the play. Like his creations in designated moments of their struggles, Milton, when introducing his play and framing its action for the reader, fails to acknowledge the existence of the relationship that he has in fact endowed with multidimensional levels of meaning. Instead he presents the reader with a world composed solely of fathers and sons.

As it is wont to do, however, the repressed returns. While beyond one early mention of "both my Parents" (26), Samson's mother disappears from Milton's story, God is represented as a mother: "I was his nursling once and choice delight," Samson explains, "His destin'd from the womb, / Promis'd by Heavenly message twice descending" (633−35). And "that self-begott'n bird" (1699), the phoenix as image of regeneration and renewal with which the Chorus counters Manoa's version of Samson's death is, of course, decisively gendered female:

> From out her ashy womb now teem'd,
> Revives, reflourishes, then vigorous most
> When most unactive deem'd,
> And though her body die, her fame survives
> A secular bird ages of lives.
>
> (1703−7)

Thus at the end of the play, Manoa and the Chorus present rival versions of heroism that compete with each other in gendered terms. As his father's insistent idealization makes clear, Samson's bringing down the pillars of the theater on himself and the Philistines represents a desirable revival (in theological and political terms) of his phallic strength; and Manoa's concluding view commands assent. In contrast, as noted earlier, for the majority of the action Samson performs his heroic identity while occupying a female position. That Milton represents Samson's female heroics as the location of significance in the play is clarified not only by the quantity of time spent focusing on this condition as the meaningful one, but also by the Chorus's eloquent valorization of heroic patience and fortitude (quoted above), that, as noted, is formulated in female terms.

I find the ending of the play unsettling and disturbing; and I am arguing that Milton concludes with two distinctively gendered heroic positions that are represented as rivals and never reconciled. This troubled (and troubling) irresolution is articulated in the frequent debates about the hero's compromised agency that run throughout the play. To what extent has he participated in his own demise, to what extent has he been helplessly betrayed, seduced and abandoned into slavery? Interestingly, in those passages where Samson contemplates himself or is contemplated as an object of seduction, the seducer is sometimes Dalila, sometimes God (e.g., 198–209, 358–61).[26] However we interpret the hero's relation to his own death—whether as a suicide or as a glorious regenerative feat—John Locke's designation of the component that clinches the definition of the slave presents an unerring description of Samson's heroic position as he lowers the pillars of the temple onto the Philistines and himself: "Whenever he finds the hardship of his slavery outweigh the value of his life, it is in his power, by resisting the will of his master, to draw on himself the death he desires. This is the perfect condition of slavery."[27] Ironically, despite his urgent glorification of Samson's masculinity, Manoa himself is responsible for complicating the gender of his son's legend by bringing him "Home to his Father's house" (1733) and turning him into a statue. Interestingly, aestheticization (often as a monument) is frequently the fate of sacrificial women in Renaissance literature.[28] We can recall that the living Samson had emphatically refused immobilization in his father's house, using contemptuous imagery of idle wifehood to underscore his resistance (566–68). Thus Samson's

final heroic position—the subject position embodying ultimate significance—is that of a woman and a slave.

III

In Aphra Behn's *Oroonoko,* the creation of the heroic position
as female and its juxtaposition with slavery are more explicitly and
centrally explored. The story presents a problematic critique of late-
seventeenth-century English colonialism, with a particular emphasis on
the slave trade. It is divided both chronologically and geographically
into two parts. The first presents the hero as an honored warrior-prince
in his African home, a country called Coramantien, where his happiness
with his beloved, Imoinda, is disrupted when the king (his grandfather)
desires Imoinda, seizes her, and eventually sells her into slavery, telling
Oroonoko she is dead. In the second half, the hero is himself sold into
slavery and is transported to the English colony Surinam, where he
meets the English narrator, joyfully discovers and reunites with Imoinda, stages a doomed rebellion, and dies.

Oroonoko was written in 1688, at a time when the project of imperial expansion and the slave trade in England were thriving. As scholars
have shown, there was an antislavery debate (although not couched in
modern terms) in the late seventeenth century; but *Oroonoko* only arguably can be called an abolitionist text.[29] As noted, the African hero
and his adored wife are both duplicitously betrayed into slavery, suffer
outrages, and die horribly trying to escape their English masters. Aristocratic Coramantiens believe that the degradation of slavery is worse
than death (e.g., 27).[30] Yet, as an African prince, Oroonoko himself
trades in and owns slaves unambivalently, as a matter of right. Laura
Rosenthal has demonstrated that slavery more often appears in this text
as a class entitlement, rather than human injustice. She argues convincingly that Behn seems to mandate the slavery practiced by the aristocratic Africans, who win their slaves in battle and trade them as part of
a gift economy that Behn sentimentally and conservatively idealizes. On
the other hand, the author's critique of English slave trading practices
takes the form of a Royalist condemnation of the greed and brazenness
characterizing the Whiggish merchant forces that propel colonialism.[31]

Moreover, the narrator's own conflicted relation to slavery disturbingly qualifies the consistency of her critique. While she struggles to escape the structures of Eurocentrism by sympathizing with Oroonoko and Imoinda and indignantly rejecting the outrages perpetrated upon them by the English, her sympathy and indignation are in fact deeply divided. The narrator's attitudes toward Oroonoko's blackness present a strong example of her ambivalence. Here is one instance of many in which she rhapsodizes about the prince's physical magnificence on one level while undercutting her praise with unacknowledged distaste on the other: "He was adorn'd with a native Beauty, so transcending all those of his gloomy Race, that he struck an Awe and Reverence, even into those that knew not his Quality; as he did into me, who beheld him with surprize and wonder, when afterwards he arrived in our World" (6).[32] *Oroonoko*, then, is a very difficult text to sort out in ideological terms. An ambivalent critique of colonialism and slavery, a Eurocentric exposure of Eurocentrism, the text is also complicated by its close relation to Behn's life and the fact that the narrator herself is clearly a surrogate for the author. By contextualizing Behn's novella among contemporary cultural narratives about slavery and women, along with the biography of Behn herself, Margaret W. Ferguson has cogently summed up these complexities: "Behn's professional and economic interests deviated just enough from those we may ascribe to England's dominant male property owners and investors in the colonies to provide a fascinating example of a female author oscillating among multiple subject positions and between complicity with and critique of the emergent institution of New World slavery."[33]

What form does heroism take in a narrative so fractured by ambivalence? In attempting to locate the heroic in Behn's text, it is useful to examine the many important ways in which *Oroonoko* resembles *Samson Agonistes*. Like Milton's play, *Oroonoko* conjoins the female subject position with slavery and compromised agency and presents the combination as the defining condition of heroism, simultaneously idealizing and scrutinizing the heroics of endurance. As in the earlier text, *Oroonoko* stakes the hero's original claim to audience attention by creating him as a traditional male military champion: "[F]rom his natural Inclination to Arms, and the Occasions given him . . . he became, at the Age of seventeen, one of the most expert Captains, and bravest Soldiers that ever saw the Field of *Mars*: so that he was ador'd as the wonder of all that World, and the Darling of the Soldiers" (6). However, the narrative does not sustain the idealization of these phallic qualities, which prove wholly inadequate and are destined never to be realized. In the African half of the story, Oroonoko's military abilities are represented rather obliquely, a point to which I'll return. In the Surinam half of the story, during his career as a slave, his identity as a hero of action, like Samson's, is reduced to performing feats like a circus strongman to amuse his captors (e.g., 50–59). Indeed, when Oroonoko stages an abortive, doomed slave rebellion, it occurs in the text directly following the narrator's account of his strongman antics (60ff). Given the hero's dignity, fierceness, and charisma in generating the rebellion, combined with his ineffectuality in pulling it off, the rebellion tends in its violent inconsequence to resemble those brave and remarkable but politically insignificant feats. Again like Samson, Oroonoko tells his secrets to a woman (the narrator), and he is (repeatedly) seduced. Further, he too occupies a female subject position, particularly when enslaved. Much of his time as a slave is spent in the narrator's household, being diverted and entertained: "He liked the Company of us Women much above the Men" (46).³⁴ Indeed Oroonoko could be seen to be enacting Samson's dreaded fantasy of being a useless wife, "idle on the household hearth." As the narrator explains when accounting for Oroonoko's agitation in captivity, "Though he suffer'd only the Name of a Slave, and had nothing of the Toil and Labour of one, yet that was sufficient to render him uneasy; and he had been too long idle, who us'd to be always in Action, and in Arms. He had a Spirit all rough and fierce, and that could not be tam'd to lazy Rest" (47). As in *Samson Agonistes,* the hero's strength proves his bane. Finally, like Samson's, Oroonoko's death bears a close and ambiguous relation to suicide.

Like Milton's, Behn's is an angry and irresolute text, rather than an elegiac one. Just as her predecessor does, Behn presents a hero with a lost past composed of high status and military achievement; and, like *Samson, Oroonoko* neither focuses intensely upon, nor mourns the disappearance of, these glories. As discussed above, in *Samson Agonistes* the hero's magnificent exploits (with the exception of the denouement) are always already over. In contrast, the structure and story of *Oroonoko* are half slave, half free, with the betrayal of the hero taking place almost exactly in the middle. Distinctly divided into two parts, in which the prince loses his country and his birthright and becomes a slave, the text would seem to present another good example of the ways in which the enslaved hero is deprived of a useable past. More interesting for purposes of this discussion, however, are the links between the subject positions the hero inhabits during his freedom and his slavery.

In contrast to Samson's original, horrific appearance in the play, Oroonoko begins as a handsome, brave, famous soldier, and he remains one for the first half of the story. While the narrator *describes* Oroonoko's valiance at length, however, most of the *dramatized* incidents represent his paralysis. The attenuation of traditional male heroics is thus applicable to both halves of the story, not simply the second, when the hero is enslaved in Surinam. His African adventures primarily concern his thwarted love for Imoinda. Oroonoko's grandfather is the king in Coramantien; enchanted by Imoinda's beauty, the impotent old man seizes her for his own while Oroonoko is off performing heroic military feats. Although the African kinship system makes it especially difficult for Oroonoko to defy his grandfather, the narrative nevertheless indicates that defiance is an option that the prince rejects: "It was objected to him, That . . . *Imoinda* being his lawful Wife by solemn Contract, 'twas he was the injur'd Man, and might, if he so pleas'd, take *Imoinda* back, the breach of the Law being on his Grandfather's side; and that if he cou'd circumvent him, and redeem her . . . it was both just and lawful for him so to do" (14). Oroonoko instead responds to Imoinda's loss by proving "pensive, and altogether unprepar'd for the Campaign . . . he lay negligently on the ground, and answer'd very little" (23). Later, he "laid himself on a Carpet, under a rich Pavilion, and remained a good while silent," vowing "that henceforth he would never lift a Weapon, or draw a bow" (27–28). The point is not that these are the conventional postures of a melancholy lover, but that Behn is interested in exploring heroic agency as paralyzed, grieved, and oppressed. Oroonoko often figures in the narrative as the passive object of the admiring, awestruck gaze (e.g., 6, 30, 39, 41). And his most frequent posture by far is not that of the valiant male conqueror, but of the female object of seduction. In Coramantien he is seduced out of his grief for Imoinda (whom his grandfather tells him is dead) and into slavery; on the slave ship he is seduced into remaining alive with lying reassurances of freedom; in Surinam he is seduced into believing that he and Imoinda will be released; into believing he won't be whipped; and into believing he will be killed, rather than forced to endure further indignities.

Oroonoko's identity as a phallic hero of action is suggestively attenuated in the African half of the novel, then; but the conditions of the heroic as Behn envisions them are starkly and unmistakably revealed during the hero's captivity in Surinam and in the manner of his death. His death occurs in an extended episode of prolonged agony, in which he leads the unsuccessful slave revolt, is deserted by all of the other slaves, kills the pregnant Imoinda in a suicide pact, then fails to kill himself and is captured, tortured, and hideously dismembered by the English colonists.

Why does Oroonoko not kill himself, rather than letting himself be killed?[35] At one point he names revenge as his motive for remaining alive after Imoinda's death (70–73); yet he neither avenges his enemies nor takes his own life. Instead he lies paralyzed by his wife's dead body, until his captors discover him. At this point, readers may find themselves wishing that the hero would release himself from further betrayal and torment. Yet, like Job, he refuses to curse God and die. We can recall that, according to Locke, the ability to commit suicide when captivity becomes intolerable is the "perfect condition of slavery." Thus by resisting suicide, Oroonoko resists self-definition as a slave. This argument is borne out by the fact that a model of the heroics of endurance which valorizes the patient suffering of unspeakable pain is twice singled out for praise by the narrator. The first instance is a description of the proud and horrifying mutilations that the warriors among the native American Indians who inhabit Surinam are seen to inflict upon themselves: "Being brought before the old Judges, now past Labour, they are ask'd, What they dare do, to shew they are worthy to lead an Army? When he who is first ask'd making no reply, cuts off his Nose, and throws it contemptibly on the ground; and the other does something to himself that he thinks surpasses him, and perhaps deprives himself of Lips and an Eye: so they slash on till one gives out, and many have dy'd in this Debate. And it's by a passive Valour they shew and prove their Activity" (58).

Stating that "For my part, I took 'em for Hobgoblins, or Fiends, rather than Men" (57), the narrator with characteristic obliquity (about which more later) assures the reader that the Indians' self-violence presents "a sort of Courage too brutal to be applauded by our *Black* Hero; nevertheless, he express'd his Esteem of 'em" (58). However, referring later to Oroonoko's own beatings, woundings, and dismemberments, she states, "I have a thousand times admired how he lived in so much tormenting Pain" (68). And as the ultimate representation of greatness, the narrator presents Oroonoko's death with admiring awe as a spectacle of the endurance of grotesque and humiliating pain:

> He had learn'd to take Tobacco; and when he was assur'd he should die, he desir'd they would give him a Pipe in his Mouth, ready lighted; which they did: And the Executioner came, and first cut off his Members, and threw them into the Fire; and after that, with an ill-favour'd Knife, they cut off his Ears and his Nose, and burn'd them; he still smoak'd on, as if nothing had touch'd him; then they hack'd off one of his Arms, and still he bore up, and held his Pipe; but at the cutting off of the other Arm, his Head sunk, and his Pipe dropt and he gave up the Ghost, without a Groan, or a Reproach. (77)

Oroonoko's heroic agency, then, is manifested in the non-suicidal (and so non-slavish) endurance of suffering; the one resolution he keeps is to "stand fix'd like a Rock, and endure Death so as should encourage [his captors] to die" (77). Yet Oroonoko *is* a slave and, being human property, cannot escape what Carole Pateman defines as "the contradiction inherent in slavery, that the humanity of the slave must necessarily be simultaneously denied and affirmed."[36] This contradiction is, of course, applicable (with some qualifications) to seventeenth-century women, who were also simultaneously considered both property and persons. Oroonoko's inscription in contradiction becomes apparent when the components of his heroism are broken down in gendered terms. The ambivalent conditions that define the heroic in this text are fully revealed when Oroonoko's destiny is compared with, and elaborated by means of, those of the two women with whom he shares the stage: Imoinda and the narrator.

As has been analyzed extensively elsewhere, the narrator's position in the text is one of discursive incoherence, particularly in her attitudes and behavior toward Oroonoko. Thus while reciting the events of the hero's death with appalled outrage, the narrator also unwittingly clarifies her own complicity in it. Although she claims a special friendship with Oroonoko and Imoinda, among the English colonists, she is the major protagonist in the plot to seduce the royal slaves from thoughts of their freedom. The narrator confides that she assured Oroonoko of his eventual freedom and then speaks with dismay of his being "fed . . . from day to day with Promises" (45), as though she were not one of the offenders. Afterward she confesses, seemingly with no sense of disparity, that she in fact spied on him and schemed against his freedom: "I was obliged, by some Persons who fear'd a Mutiny . . . to discourse with [him] and to give him all the Satisfaction I possibly could" (46); and that she came to mistrust him: "I neither thought it convenient to trust him much out of our view, nor did the Country, who fear'd him" (48); and, later, "We were possess'd with extreme Fear, which no Persuasions could dissipate, that he would secure himself till night, and then, that he would come down and cut all our Throats" (68). Finally, seemingly (and oddly) to exonerate herself, she confesses to abandoning him twice, in instances when he is tortured and at last killed: "For I suppose I had Authority and Interest enough there, had I suspected any such thing, to have prevented it" (68).[37]

Oroonoko and the narrator, then, each possess compromised and strained agency. As noted, Oroonoko is paralyzed by the obvious contradiction that, like a woman, a slave is property while simultaneously remaining a human being. The narrator implicitly recognizes her connections to the hero when she links what she considers to be the inferiority of her female authorship with Oroonoko's destiny as a slave. For example, at exactly the point (40) when the hero is renamed "Caesar" (being renamed and so possessed is the fate of women and slaves) she remarks, "His Misfortune was, to fall in an obscure World, that afforded only a Female Pen to celebrate his Fame." In the final words of the story, she announces cryptically, "Thus died this great Man, worthy of a better Fate, and a more sublime Wit than mine to write his Praise" (78). However, though identifying with the female position of the slave, the narrator, as discussed above, also identifies with and participates in the European structures that oppress him and, presumably, herself.

Like the narrator, the hero is both slave and slave-master. While his position as an owner is explicit before he himself becomes a slave, Oroonoko enacts his conflicted identity with painful clarity when he kills his wife. As scholars like Patterson have pointed out, one of the characteristics of slavery is the slave's lack of control over kinship ties.[38] In this sense, as Charlotte Sussman cogently argues, Oroonoko's killing of Imoinda, which also includes aborting their child, proves an act of mastery, a resistance to slavery. The gruesomely ironic fact—that Oroonoko can assert mastery only in this destructive and self-destructive sense—of course points in a circular fashion back to his slavery. Sussman makes the interesting point that Oroonoko acts out this duality when confronting his captors over his wife's dead body: cutting flesh from his own throat, he imitates slitting Imoinda's; disemboweling himself, he "recalls that he has just effectively aborted Imoinda's child. . . . Thus, the sign of Oroonoko's courage to choose a noble death over the shame of slavery is also a repetition of the sign of his absolute possession of wife and child." Yet, "the code of nobility that Oroonoko writes on his own body signifies his power over a woman, not his emancipation from slavery."[39]

If the ambivalent conditions characterizing Oroonoko's identity and agency as owner and slave are displaced onto the white female narrator, so too does Imoinda enact displaced parts of her husband's heroic identity: namely, his slavery. Like the narrator's, Imoinda's explicitly female destiny clarifies the multiple meanings of the heroics of endurance. As Ferguson and Sussman have made clear, it is the black slave / wife who unambiguously bears the symbolic brunt of powerlessness in the text. At critical points in the narrative (e.g., during the slave revolt) Imoinda shows herself capable of courageous deeds; she is the only slave who attacks a white male ruler. Indeed, Ferguson has argued convincingly for a causal relation between Imoinda's physical courage and her death.[40] But the major significance of her actions is her willingness to die at her husband's hands, a scene which the narrator describes as follows: "He told her his Design, first of killing her, and then his Enemies, and next himself, and the Impossibility of escaping, and therefore he told her the

Necessity of dying. He found the heroick Wife faster pleading for Death, than he was to propose it, when she found his fix'd Resolution . . . for Wives have a respect for their Husbands equal to what any other People pay a Deity" (71–72).

When describing Imoinda's marriage, the narrator romanticizes her subordinate condition as accepted without ambivalence, even joyfully. But Behn also directly connects the violence that defines all slavery with Imoinda's sexuality, including, by implicit extension, female sexuality in general. In Africa, kidnapped by the doting grandfather, Imoinda occupies the status of possession even before she literally becomes a slave. We have already seen how her death at her husband's hand embodies all the tragic ironies of slavery. There is also an earlier, very telling conflation of violence, female sexuality, and slavery. After his capture, Oroonoko befriends his owner, Trefry, and, learning that Trefry is suffering from unrequited love of a slave and not yet knowing that the slave is Imoinda, Oroonoko asks Trefry why he does not simply rape the object of his desires. Trefry replies, " 'I have been ready to make use of those Advantages of Strength and Force Nature has given me: But Oh! she disarms me with that Modesty and Weeping, so tender and so moving, that I retire and thank my Stars she overcame me.' The Company laugh'd at his Civility to a Slave" (42–43).

IV

With this conflation of the woman / wife and the slave as vulnerable to sexual violence, Aphra Behn represents male dominance based on physical strength as a figure for all oppression. While in Behn's text the conjunction is implicitly articulated and ambivalently qualified in multifaceted representations, in Mary Astell's *Some Reflections upon Marriage,* the conflation of the woman / wife and the slave is directly and systematically developed in impassioned polemic. As noted, Behn manages with self-serving sentimentality to sever the single white woman narrator's more powerful position from that of the black, married slave; further, in Behn's narrative structure Imoinda's story is crucial, but decentered. Astell's text is also divided, between a single woman narrator (in this case Astell herself) who is not disempowered and a married woman who is by Astell's definition a slave. But in Astell's text, the wife / slave is the central figure. No longer displaced, no longer meta-phorical, her identity is now literal; she has become the hero.

If the defining condition of slavery is that it presents the only alter-native to death, then the conflation of the wife and the slave could be seen as structurally imperfect. Locke, for example, argues that the pub-lic and private spheres are distinguished precisely by the fact that the husband, *unlike* the sovereign, does not possess the power of life and death over his wife.[41] Nevertheless, Patterson's analysis of the slave as a "social nonperson," or Pateman's of the wife and the slave as each civilly dead, demonstrate the power and cogency of the analogy when ex-tended beyond the literal. Like Milton, when defining the configura-tions of power and desire in marriage, Astell draws on decades of Protestant discourse that analogizes marriage to the state, linking the public and private spheres. Interestingly, when defining the married woman in no uncertain terms as a slave, Astell attacks Milton:

> Patience and Submission are the only Comforts that are left to a poor People, who groan under Tyranny, unless they are Strong enough to break the Yoke, to Depose and Abdicate, which I doubt wou'd not be allow'd of here [i.e., in marriage]. For whatever may be said against Passive-Obedience in another case, I suppose there's no Man but likes it very well in this; how much soever Arbitrary Power may be dislik'd on a Throne, Not *Milton* himself wou'd cry up Liberty to poor *Female Slaves,* or plead for the Lawfulness of Resisting a Private Tyranny. (28–29)[42]

Astell and Milton are political opposites: he is a Puritan radical and regicide who, despite ambivalence about hierarchy, buttresses male su-periority; she is a conservative, monarchist, high Anglican Tory who (in-consistently, given her use of the family / state analogy) protests male superiority in the private sphere.[43] Interestingly, just as they do in *Samson Agonistes,* the contradictions in *Some Reflections* emerge through the representation of the problematic concept of wifely obedience. (As we have seen, in Behn's text this tricky issue is romanticized and its contra-dictions self-consciously erased.)

Although she concludes her polemic with an idealized version of heroic female patience, in the passage quoted above Astell is not recom-mending obedience and patience as heroic, but rather is defining them as limiting, indicating lack of empowerment. The mixed message is forcefully apparent in her consideration of the constraints on female agency. On the one hand, she argues that women have no agency in the marriage market: "A Woman indeed can't properly be said to Choose, all that is allow'd her, is to Refuse or Accept what is offer'd" (23). On the other hand, Astell herself has pointedly chosen *not* to marry. And in later sections of her essay, she asserts that women do have a choice in the selection of mates:

> She who Elects a Monarch for Life, who gives him an Authority she cannot recall however he misapply it, who puts her Fortune and Person entirely in his Power; nay even the very desires of her Heart according to some learned Casuists, so as that it is not lawful to Will or Desire any thing but what he approves and allows, had need be very sure that she does not make a Fool her Head, nor a Vicious Man her Guide and Pattern, she had best stay till she can meet with one who has the Government of his own Passions and has duly regulated his own Desires, since he is to have such an absolute Power over hers. (32–33)

This hypothesis of a good husband in effect deconstructs itself, as Astell dwells so insistently on the unequal power relationships that define marriage. Notably, no examples of good marriages appear in the text. Also, Astell employs the traditional feminist argument that women suffer not from essential, gendered inferiority, but from lack of an education and the options it introduces: "But, alas! what poor Woman is ever taught that she should have a higher Design than to get her a Husband?" (66). After marriage, a woman "has nothing else to do but to Please and Obey" (59); further, "she who can't do this is no way fit to be a Wife" (60). The not-so-sub-text of this analysis is that, given the construction of marriage as a tyranny, no woman is fit to be a wife. To put this proposition another way, wifehood is not suitable for any woman.

Why, then, do women consistently go about surrendering the little agency they have, however compromised, in order to get married? That men and women should be erotically drawn to one another simply is not a possibility for Astell. Sexual desire, so critical and passionately destructive in Milton's text and Behn's, becomes trivial, foolish, vain delusion in Astell's. In her most ferocious foray against the heroics of endurance, she exposes the connection between passive obedience and seduction. She delivers a brilliant, devastating attack on courtship as idolatrous and deceptive, designed to induct women into a life of servitude: "[H]e may call himself her Slave a few days, but it is only in order to make her his all the rest of his Life" (25). With dramatically restrained rage, Astell presents a most unrelenting exposure of the contempt for women that lies behind male courtship, with its abstract, insistent idealizations: "For nothing is in truth a greater outrage than Flattery and feign'd Submissions, the plain English of which is this; . . . 'We who make the Idols, are the greater Deities; and as we set you up, so it is in our power to reduce you to your first obscurity, or to somewhat worse, to Contempt'" (25–26). In imagery that recalls *Samson Agonistes,* she concludes that "a Blind Obedience is what a Rational Creature shou'd never Pay" (87).

Astell's analysis of the dynamics of seduction leads her, like Milton and Behn, to recognize physical strength as the misguided source of male dominance. Rather than mourning male valor as sadly lost, she attacks the idea of the supposed superiority of male strength with unspeakable, classist glee:

> It were ridiculous to suppose that a Woman, were she ever so much improv'd, cou'd come near the topping Genius of the Men, and therefore why shou'd they envy or discourage her? Strength of Mind goes along with Strength of Body, and 'tis only for some odd accidents which Philosophers have not yet thought worth while to enquire into, that the Sturdiest Porter is not the Wisest Man. As therefore the Men have the Power in their Hands, so there's no dispute of their having the Brains to manage it. . . . Do not they generally speaking do all the great Actions and considerable Business of this World, and leave that of the next to the Women? . . . Justice and Injustice are administered by their Hands, Courts and Schools are fill'd with these Sages; . . . Histories are writ by them, they recount each others great Exploits, and have always done so. . . . Indeed what is it they can't perform, when they attempt it? (91–92)

Having thoroughly undercut the traditional bases of the male heroics of action, Astell has little choice but to propose an alternative subjectivity grounded in endurance, a heroism that is distinctly female:

"For she . . . who can be so truly mortify'd as to lay aside her own Will and Desires, to pay such an entire Submission for Life, to one whom she cannot be sure will always deserve it, does certainly perform a more Heroic Action than all the famous Masculine Heroes can boast of" (93). Yet Astell's exposure of the humiliating, oppressive, and compromising conditions defining this martyrdom has been potent enough to mitigate its claims for approval. At one point she does envision equality between the sexes, although interestingly not in the marriage relation, but in the public sphere: "She will discern a time when her Sex shall be no bar to the best Employments, the highest Honor . . . provided she is not wanting to her self, her Soul shall shine as bright as the greatest Hero's" (88).

V

Astell does not develop this visionary insight. Like Milton's and Behn's, her argument implies that only revolutions can change the existing interrelations of gender and power; and, like Milton and Behn, she finds that revolutions fail. Like *Samson Agonistes* and *Oroonoko, Some Reflections upon Marriage* is a text extraordinary for its anger and despair. All three texts begin with the premise that the heroics of action is ineffectual, outdated; and none mourns the demise of traditional, phallic glory as the legitimate form of the heroic. Instead, all three propose an alternative heroics of endurance, that, while idealized with varying intensity in each, is shown in all to incur terrible costs. Indeed this heroism is presented at best as ambivalent and compromised, at worst as bitter and scathing. Elaborated in terms of seduction, marriage, and slavery, the heroic attains its purest form in Astell's text, when the wife and the slave literally become the same person, who is also the figure of major significance: the hero. Each text presents a central figure who is seduced into slavery and paralyzed, caught between being identified with, and opposed to, other central figures. This contradictory position, conflated in each case with slavery, is also and always a female position, the position of the woman. In *Samson Agonistes, Oroonoko,* and *Some Reflections upon Marriage,* it becomes the situation of the hero, forming the combination of factors that defines and constitutes heroic experience.

Epilogue

In this study of gender and heroism in early modern England, I have tried to suggest some new ways to think about the interrelationship of texts, change over time, and the role representation plays in a culture's evaluation of itself. The analysis moves in two directions: first, it provides an account of transforming models of heroism from the late sixteenth to the late seventeenth centuries; second it offers a critique of heroic representation and meaning.

Rather than assessing heroism in terms of character and action, I have defined it abstractly, as a position in a textual structure. Heroism, I argue, is a space into which a culture projects its idealizations, and, as such, designates meaning and determines value. I have tried to show that the gendering of heroism from the late sixteenth to the late seventeenth centuries powerfully registers cultural change. I trace a process of transformation in which the active male heroism of rule, exploration, and conquest that predominates at the beginning of the period I study gives way to a heroism that valorizes the patient suffering of disaster and pain. Viewing heroism as a position in a structure opens the possibility that that position can be inhabited by individual, gendered agents. By the late seventeenth century, the dominant heroic mode is defined in terms of endurance more than action and is constituted in terms that resemble those in which early modern women are idealized; therefore the heroics of endurance is open to women as well as men. It becomes clear that actual men and women as well as male and female protagonists in texts can be and are heroes, and that significance itself is not always associated with or located in masculinity. Indeed heroism for both women and men comes to be constituted through its enabling relation to positions, capacities, virtues, and values usually associated with women and femininity.

The male heroics of action of course survives as a Western cultural

113

model; but in the Renaissance it begins to lose its attachment to contemporary historical necessities and therefore its dominance. As noted in the prologue, this development can be explained historically by summoning the usual suspects. The centralization of the nation-state and the state's effort to monopolize violence; the change from a land-based to a money economy and the consequent alterations in class predominance and increased opportunities for social mobility; the success of Protestantism: these long-range and well-documented phenomena combine virtually to assure that literary idealizations will transform. Critic Northrop Frye once observed that great tragedy appears when an aristocracy is losing its power while at the same time retaining its prestige.[1] The aristocratic warrior heroes of Shakespeare's late tragedies clarify Frye's point: their glamorous and failed destinies are all rooted in an identification with a militaristic masculinity dramatized as impossibly lost. As a literary form tragedy lends seriousness and dignity as well as elegy to its themes: the aspiring dominance of the male heroism of action is mourned and lamented; the future will be a diminished thing.

Responding to the power and beauty of Renaissance tragedies, scholars have often absorbed and reproduced this nostalgic scenario of decline and diminishment when discussing other literary forms, particularly at the end of the seventeenth century. But a view of heroic representation as sadly declining in energy and power throughout the century can only be sustained if heroism is defined exclusively as active, aristocratic, and male. I hope my analysis has convinced readers of the inaccuracies and limitations of this view of the heroic. Recent scholarship has clarified the multiplicity and fluidity of available subject positions in early modern England both positively, by taking gender into account, and negatively, by not assuming that prescriptive norms successfully stabilize human behavior, either in literary representation or in actual life experience. Building on this research, I have argued that Renaissance heroes do not simply attempt to consolidate an aggressive masculinity through violence; rather they seek omnipotence by endeavoring to monopolize all dominant subject positions, which are, inevitably, gendered. Further, even the most insistently masculinist writers, like Marlowe and Jonson, place their heroes in female subject positions that are both necessary and desired, although that necessity and desire often remain unacknowledged in retrospect in the service of retaining the appearance of stable masculine dominance. Elizabeth I also seeks omnipotence; but in contrast to Renaissance male heroes, she recognizes the prestige of both female and male subject positions and openly inhabits a variety of gendered positions when establishing her rhetoric of heroism.

As is well known, the ideological transformations of the seventeenth century include a self-conscious effort in many cultural domains to consolidate the heretofore more blurred discursive boundaries between the genders and, correspondingly, between the public and private spheres. Until recently some feminist scholars have treated the separation of the spheres as a narrative of decline and diminishment for women, viewing female agency as increasingly constrained by the confinement of women to the private sphere that is associated with bourgeois ascendancy.[2] Whatever gains and losses may be seen as accompanying these processes of cultural change, it is crucial to my analysis that in the early modern period a newly defined private sphere emerges as an arena for human heroism, and that heroism is constructed predominantly in terms that are gendered female. During the sixteenth century Elizabeth I's refusal to marry exhibits an adamant belief (implicitly shared by Parliament) that public heroism is incompatible with women and with private life. In contrast, by the end of the seventeenth century, Milton, summing up almost two hundred years of Protestant commentary, vehemently argues both in his poetic fictions and his prose tracts for the heroic significance of marriage and private life. As I have demonstrated, that heroism privileges endurance and passive suffering and is constructed in terms that resemble the early modern idealization of women.

That there should be a gender-based conflict about the meaning and place of action and suffering in the public and private realms is already apparent in Elizabeth's persistent struggles to remain unmarried, which not only are enacted in her public speeches but become a constituent part of her heroism. Yet for Elizabeth this potential conflict is one theme among many; her status allows her to avoid living it out as much as is possible. In contrast, the four female autobiographers I consider are ordinary women rather than queens. In texts written decades later, after the revolution, the conflict these writers experience between prescribed roles for women and the self-assertion their circumstances require becomes the shaping factor of their life accounts and the condition of their heroism. Female heroism thus emerges as conflicted and problematic, constituted as constrained and compromised agency. These are the very conditions that come to characterize modern heroism as a whole, represented in both male and female figures and in texts authored by both men and women.

By considering the changing interrelation of gender and heroism in early modern England, this book revalues what has been assumed, historically at least, to be a male monopoly on cultural status and prestige. But this study will have missed its aim if it seems to be celebrating the eventual replacement of the male-defined heroism of action by a heroism of endurance that can be understood best as female. Studying the heroic can be a distressing process, and I mean this book to be a critique of both idealized domination and idealized suffering. By viewing the heroic as a location of meaningfulness rather than as a description of character or action, I have tried to complicate certain moral and psychological assumptions traditionally associated with heroism. My analysis assumes throughout that the process of assigning significance to persons and events has important political implications, particularly in the accumulation and distribution of cultural capital. Glamour and prestige attach to both male and female heroes, and heroic deeds, whether of action or suffering, often incur collective gratitude, along with material and symbolic rewards. But my analysis questions whether cultural idealizations that command prestige inevitably are positive or desirable; or whether a hero must be by definition brave, superior, or self-sacrificing; or whether self-sacrifice is inherently an altruistic or benevolent, rather than a violent, often suicidal enterprise.

Heroism most often represents reality as a choice between life and death. The disturbing aspect of these options for me is the frequency with which they issue in violence. In early modern England the politics of literary form place a premium on tragedy and epic, genres that confer dignity and respect on violence, self-sacrifice, and death. But choice itself is also a necessary part of the heroic terrain. Embedded in both the heroics of endurance and the heroics of action is the option of survival, a heroism represented in this book by Elizabeth I and the four women autobiographers. As the career of Odysseus makes clear, there have

been male as well as female heroic survivors throughout Western literature. Their wit, resourcefulness, patience, stubbornness, generosity
and sheer tenacity are usually given comic treatment. While it is generally more loved, comedy (wrongly in my view) often is considered to be
a less dignified, less serious literary form. But what if the assignment of
prestige were the other way around? It comes down to a matter of cultural politics; it is, after all, a matter of choice.

Notes

Prologue

1. Traditional sources for this idea include Alice Clark's *Working Life of Women in the Seventeenth Century* (1919; reprint, London: Routledge and Kegan Paul, 1982); and Joan Kelly's pathbreaking essay, "Did Women Have a Renaissance?" in *Women, History, and Theory: The Essays of Joan Kelly* (Chicago: University of Chicago Press, 1984), 19–50. More recent examples, among many, of scholarship that richly mines the separate spheres narrative include Carole Pateman, *The Sexual Contract* (Stanford, Calif.: Stanford University Press, 1988); Thomas A. Laqueur, *Making Sex: Body and Gender from the Greeks to Freud* (Cambridge, Mass.: Harvard University Press, 1990); and Jodi Mikalachki, *The Legacy of Boadicea: Gender and Nation in Early Modern England* (London: Routledge, 1998). Both Pateman and Mikalachki emphasize the explicit, self-conscious articulation of gendered separate spheres in John Locke.

2. See, for example, Amy Louise Erickson, *Women and Property in Early Modern England* (London: Routledge, 1993); and Robert B. Shoemaker, *Gender in English Society, 1650–1850: The Emergence of Separate Spheres?* (London: Addison Wesley Longman Limited, 1998). Shoemaker provides an excellent synthesis of the formulation and development of the separate spheres argument, which he questions and nuances, but also upholds.

3. All quotations from Shakespeare come from *The Norton Shakespeare*, ed. Stephen Greenblatt, Walter Cohen, Jean E. Howard, and Katherine Eisaman Maus (New York: W. W. Norton, 1997), and are cited in the text by act, scene, and line numbers. All quotations from Milton are from John Milton, *Complete Poems and Major Prose*, ed. Merritt Y. Hughes (Indianapolis, Ind.: Odyssey, 1957), and are cited in the text by book, sonnet, and line numbers.

4. Norbert Elias, *The Civilizing Process: The History of Manners* and *State Formation and Civilization*, trans. Edmund Jephcott (Oxford: Blackwell, 1994), 388. For other studies of the formation of nation-states in the West, see Benedict Anderson, *Imagined Communities: Reflections on the Origin and Spread of Nationalism* (London: Verso, 1996); and Richard Helgerson, *Forms of Nationhood: The Elizabethan Writing of England* (Chicago: University of Chicago Press, 1992). For connections between nationalism and gender and/or private life, see Mikalachki, *Legacy of Boadicea*; and Jack Goody, *The Development of the Family and Marriage in Europe* (Cambridge, Eng.: Cambridge University Press, 1983).

5. Most of these analyses are inspired by Michel Foucault, *Discipline and Punish: The Birth of the Prison*, trans. Alan Sheridan (New York: Vintage Books, 1979). For discussions relating particularly to early modern English literature and culture, see Stephen Greenblatt,

119

"Invisible Bullets," in *Shakespearean Negotiations: Circulations of Social Energy in Renaissance England* (Berkeley: University of California Press, 1988), 21–65; Steven Mullaney, "Lying Like Truth: Riddle, Representation, and Treason in Renaissance England," *ELH* 47 (1980): 32–74; Karen Cunningham, "Renaissance Execution and Marlovian Elocution: The Drama of Death," *PMLA* 105 (1990): 209–22; and Frances E. Dolan, "'Gentlemen, I have one thing more to say': Women on Scaffolds in England, 1563–1680," *Modern Philology* 92.2 (1994): 157–78.

6.   Michael Murrin, *History and Warfare in Renaissance Epic* (Chicago: University of Chicago Press, 1994). Also see Arthur B. Ferguson, *The Indian Summer of English Chivalry: Studies in the Decline and Transformation of Chivalric Idealism* (Durham, N.C.: Duke University Press, 1960); and Maurice Keen, *Chivalry* (New Haven, Conn.: Yale University Press, 1984).

7.   See Lawrence Stone, *The Crisis of the Aristocracy, 1558–1641* (Oxford: Clarendon, 1965), and "Social Mobility in England, 1500–1700," *Past and Present* 33 (1966): 16–55; Keith Wrightson, *English Society, 1580–1680* (New Brunswick, N.J.: Rutgers University Press, 1982); Peter Laslett, *The World We Have Lost: England before the Industrial Age* (New York: Scribner's, 1965); Frank Whigham, *Ambition and Privilege: The Social Tropes of Elizabethan Courtesy Theory* (Berkeley: University of California Press, 1984); and Richard Halperin, *The Poetics of Primitive Accumulation: English Renaissance Culture and the Genealogy of Capital* (Ithaca, N.Y.: Cornell University Press, 1991).

8.   Elias, *State Formation and Civilization,* 412.

9.   Ibid., 403.

10.   Alexander Niccholes, *A Discourse of Marriage and Wiving* (London, 1615), 164, 159, 161. For a full discussion of the heroics of marriage, see Mary Beth Rose, *The Expense of Spirit: Love and Sexuality in English Renaissance Drama* (Ithaca, N.Y.: Cornell University Press, 1988), 116–31.

11.   Niccholes, *Discourse of Marriage,* 159.

12.   William Whately, *A Care-cloth* (London, 1624), 80.

13.   William Gouge, *Of Domesticall Duties* (London, 1622), 378.

14.   Gouge, *Domesticall Duties,* 378.

15.   Whately, *Care-cloth,* 80–82.

16.   The best study of heroism in pre- and early modern Western literature, and one to which I am greatly indebted, remains Reuben A. Brower, *Hero and Saint: Shakespeare and the Graeco-Roman Heroic Tradition* (New York: Oxford University Press, 1971).

17.   Judith Butler, *Bodies That Matter: On the Discursive Limits of "Sex"* (New York: Routledge, 1993), 5, 10, 12, 14, 16. Cf. Daniel Boyarin, *Unheroic Conduct: The Rise of Heterosexuality and the Invention of the Jewish Man* (Berkeley: University of California Press, 1997), 85: "Models function not so much as programs for construction as strategies of disavowing the inconsistencies of constructions."

18.   Boyarin, *Unheroic Conduct,* 57. Lower-class characters are generally excluded from heroism, almost by definition. However, Tamburlaine (a creation of Marlowe's radical imagination) immediately springs to mind as an exception. More often, non-aristocratic heroes are characters of uncertain class status: are Deloney's Jack of Newbury and Dekker's Simon Eyre middle class, or of the "middling sort"?

19.   Throughout her book, *Dangerous Familiars: The Representation of Domestic Crime in*

England, 1550–1700 (Ithaca, N.Y.: Cornell University Press, 1994), Frances E. Dolan has many insightful discussions of the relation between female agency and violence.

20. Jonathan Goldberg, *Sodometries* (Stanford, Calif.: Stanford University Press, 1992), 205.

21. See, for example, Boyarin, *Unheroic Conduct*; Goldberg, *Sodometries*; Valerie Traub, *Desire and Anxiety: Circulations of Sexuality in Shakespearean Drama* (London: Routledge, 1992); Jeffrey Masten, *Textual Intercourse: Collaboration, Authorship, and Sexualities in Renaissance Drama* (Cambridge, Eng.: Cambridge University Press, 1997); Mario Di Gangi, *The Homoerotics of Early Modern Drama* (Cambridge, Eng.: Cambridge University Press, 1997); Mark Breitenberg, *Anxious Masculinity in Early Modern England* (Cambridge, Eng.: Cambridge University Press, 1996); Gregory Bredbeck, *Sodomy and Interpretation: Marlowe to Milton* (Ithaca, N.Y.: Cornell University Press, 1991); Bruce R. Smith, *Homosexual Desire in Shakespeare's England: A Cultural Poetics* (Chicago: University of Chicago Press, 1991); and Jonathan Goldberg, ed., *Queering the Renaissance* (Durham, N.C.: Duke University Press, 1994).

22. See Leah S. Marcus, Janel Mueller, and Mary Beth Rose, eds., *Elizabeth I: Collected Works* (Chicago: University of Chicago Press, 2000).

23. Constance Jordan, *Renaissance Feminism: Literary Texts and Political Models* (Ithaca, N.Y.: Cornell University Press, 1990); and Maureen Quilligan, *The Allegory of Female Authority: Christine de Pizan's* Cité des Dames (Ithaca, N.Y.: Cornell University Press, 1991).

Chapter One

1. Sigmund Freud, "The Relation of the Poet to Day-Dreaming," in *Character and Culture* (New York: Collier Books, 1963), 40.

2. All quotations from *Tamburlaine*, identified in the text by part, act, scene, and line numbers, come from Russell A. Fraser and Norman Rabkin, eds., *Drama of the English Renaissance*, vol. 1, *The Tudor Period* (New York: Macmillan, 1976), 207–61.

3. Much of the discussion of *Tamburlaine* up to this point in the chapter comes from Mary Beth Rose, *The Expense of Spirit: Love and Sexuality in English Renaissance Drama* (Ithaca, N.Y.: Cornell University Press, 1988), 105–10.

4. For a helpful discussion of the association of women with ornamentation, see Howard Bloch, "Medieval Misogyny," *Representations* 20 (1987): 1–24.

5. Christopher Pye, *The Regal Phantasm: Shakespeare and the Politics of Spectacle* (London: Routledge, 1990), 4.

6. Ibid., 44.

7. For two particularly good analyses of this narrative structure, see Teresa de Lauretis, *Alice Doesn't: Feminism, Semiotics, Cinema* (Bloomington: Indiana University Press, 1984), esp. 103–57; and Mary Jacobus, *Reading Woman: Essays in Feminist Criticism* (New York: Columbia University Press, 1986), 83–193.

8. Timothy Reiss, *Tragedy and Truth: Studies in the Development of a Renaissance and Neoclassical Discourse* (New Haven: Yale University Press, 1980), 103–33.

9. See Marion Wynne-Davies, "'The Swallowing Womb': Consumed and Consuming in *Titus Andronicus*," in *The Matter of Difference: Materialist Feminist Criticism of Shakespeare*, ed. Valerie Wayne (Ithaca, N.Y.: Cornell University Press, 1991), 129–51. Also see Patricia Francis Cholakian, *Rape and Writing in the* Heptaméron *of Marguerite de Navarre* (Carbondale,

Ill.: Southern Illinois University Press, 1991), esp. 117; and Frances E. Dolan, *Dangerous Familiars: Representations of Domestic Crime in England, 1550–1700* (Ithaca, N.Y.: Cornell University Press, 1994), 102–41.

10. The quotation from *Epicoene* is from Fraser and Rabkin, *Drama of the English Renaissance*, vol. 2, *The Stuart Period*, 4.1.90.

11. Quotations from *Dr. Faustus*, identified in the text by act, scene, and line numbers, come from Fraser and Rabkin, *Drama of the English Renaissance*, vol. 1, *The Tudor Period*, 297–322. *Dr. Faustus* is a play with notorious textual difficulties. There are two texts, A (1604) and B (1616), and the A text is now generally preferred. To study the differences between the two texts, readers should consult the superb edition of the play which presents them separately, edited by David Bevington and Eric Rasmussen (Manchester, Eng.: Manchester University Press, 1993). See especially 62–77, which present a textual analysis. I have indicated in the text of my discussion when I quote lines that appear only in the B text.

12. See Jacques Lacan, *The Four Fundamental Concepts of Psycho-analysis*, ed. Jacques-Alain Miller and trans. Alan Sheridan (New York: W. W. Norton, 1981), esp. 69–91 and 257.

13. See Leonard Barkan, *The Gods Made Flesh: Metamorphosis and the Pursuit of Paganism* (New Haven, Conn.: Yale University Press, 1986), 191ff, for an account of various traditions surrounding the figure of Danae, including one in which she is figured as the Virgin Mary.

14. See, for one relatively recent example, Stephen Greenblatt, "Marlowe and the Will to Absolute Play," in *Renaissance Self-Fashioning: From More to Shakespeare* (Chicago: University of Chicago Press, 1980), 193–221.

15. James Shapiro, *Rival Playwrights: Marlowe, Jonson, Shakespeare* (New York: Columbia University Press, 1991), 39–73.

16. See, for example, Anne Barton, *Ben Jonson, Dramatist* (Cambridge, Eng.: Cambridge University Press, 1984), 105–19; and Jonas Barish, *The Antitheatrical Prejudice* (Berkeley: University of California Press, 1981), 146–47.

17. All citations from *Volpone*, identified in the text by act, scene, and line numbers, come from Fraser and Rabkin, *Drama of the English Renaissance*, vol. 2, *The Stuart Period*, 57–99.

18. See the now classic essay by Nancy Vickers, "Diana Described: Scattered Woman and Scattered Rhyme," in *Writing and Sexual Difference*, ed. Elizabeth Abel (Chicago: University of Chicago Press, 1982), 95–109.

19. For an elegant discussion of the relationship between alienation and the representation of violence in Marlowe, see Karen Cunningham, "Renaissance Execution and Marlovian Elocution: The Drama of Death," *PMLA* 105 (1990): 209–22.

20. All quotations from *Macbeth, Antony and Cleopatra,* and *Coriolanus* are from *The Norton Shakespeare,* eds. Stephen Greenblatt, Walter Cohen, Jean E. Howard, and Katherine Eisaman Maus (New York: W. W. Norton, 1997) and are cited in the text by act, scene, and line numbers.

21. See Rose, *Expense of Spirit,* 131–55.

22. Janet Adelman, *Suffocating Mothers: Fantasies of Maternal Origin in Shakespeare's Plays,* Hamlet *to* The Tempest (New York: Routledge, 1992), 147–64.

23. Ibid., 130–47.

Chapter Two

1. See J. E. Neale, *Elizabeth I and Her Parliaments: 1559–1581* (New York: W. W. Norton, 1958) and *Elizabeth I and Her Parliaments: 1584–1601* (London: Cape, 1957).

2. See, for example, Christopher Haigh, ed., *The Reign of Elizabeth I* (Athens: University of Georgia Press, 1985) and *Elizabeth I* (London: Longman, 1988); and Julia M. Walker, ed., *Dissing Elizabeth: Negative Representations of Gloriana* (Durham, N.C.: Duke University Press, 1998).

3. Leah S. Marcus, Janel Mueller, and Mary Beth Rose, eds., *Elizabeth I: Collected Works* (Chicago: University of Chicago Press, 2000). See the preface, in which the rationale for the editorial decisions is explained in detail. All quotations from Elizabeth's speeches come from this edition and are documented in the text by page numbers.

4. See George P. Rice Jr., ed., *The Public Speaking of Queen Elizabeth: Selections from Her Official Addresses* (New York: Columbia University Press, 1951); and Neale, *Elizabeth I and Her Parliaments, 1559–1581* and *Elizabeth I and Her Parliaments, 1584–1601*. For a recent biography based on Elizabeth's utterances, see Maria Perry, *The Word of a Prince: A Life of Elizabeth I from Contemporary Documents* (Woodbridge, Eng.: Boydell, 1990). For an early analysis of the texts of the speeches, see Allison Heisch, "Queen Elizabeth I: Parliamentary Rhetoric and the Exercise of Power," *Signs* 1 (Autumn 1975): 31–55.

5. See the preface to Marcus, Mueller, and Rose, *Collected Works*, xi–xxiv.

6. Frances Yates, *Astraea: The Imperial Theme in the Sixteenth Century* (London: Routledge, 1975); Roy Strong, *The Cult of Elizabeth: Elizabethan Portraiture and Pageantry* (Berkeley: University of California Press, 1977); John Nichols, ed., *The Progresses and Public Processions of Queen Elizabeth*, 3 vols. (London: J. Nichols and Son, 1823; reprint, New York: AMS Press, n.d.); Philippa Berry, *Of Chastity and Power: Elizabethan Literature and the Unmarried Queen* (London: Routledge, 1989); Helen Hackett, *Virgin Mother, Maiden Queen: Elizabeth I and the Cult of the Virgin Mary* (New York: St. Martin's, 1995); Susan Frye, *Elizabeth I: The Competition for Representation* (New York: Oxford University Press, 1993); Carole Levin, *The Heart and Stomach of a King: Elizabeth I and the Politics of Sex and Power* (Philadelphia: University of Pennsylvania Press, 1994); and Marie Axton, *The Queen's Two Bodies: Drama and the Elizabethan Succession* (London: Royal Historical Society, 1977). The Montrose quotation is from "The Elizabethan Subject and the Spenserian Text," in *Literary Theory / Renaissance Texts*, ed. Patricia Parker and David Quint (Baltimore: Johns Hopkins University Press, 1986), 306.

7. Montrose, "Elizabethan Subject," 310.

8. Frye, *Competition for Representation*, 7.

9. For discussion of the debates about female rule in the English Renaissance, see Mortimer Levine, "The Place of Women in Tudor Government," in *Tudor Rule and Revolution: Essays for G. R. Elton from His American Friends*, ed. Delloyd J. Guth and John W. McKenna (Cambridge: Cambridge University Press, 1982), 109–23; Constance Jordan, "Woman's Rule in Sixteenth-Century British Political Thought," *Renaissance Quarterly* 40 (1987): 421–51, and *Renaissance Feminism: Literary Texts and Political Models* (Ithaca, N.Y.: Cornell University Press, 1990); Paula Louise Scalingi, "The Scepter or the Distaff: The Question of Female Sovereignty, 1516–1607," *The Historian* 41 (1978): 59–75; James E. Phillips Jr., "The Back-

ground of Spenser's Attitude toward Women Rulers," *Huntington Library Quarterly* 5 (1941), 5–32; and Levin, *Heart and Stomach of a King,* 10–16.

10. John Knox, *Works,* ed. David Laing (Edinburgh: James Thin, 1895), 4: 369.

11. John Aylmer, *An Harborrowe for Faithfull and Trewe Subjectes* (London: J. Daye, 1559), n.p.

12. Variations in these arguments are made in, among other places, the sources listed in note 6. See also Christine Coch, "'Mother of my Contreye': Elizabeth I and Tudor Constructions of Motherhood," *English Literary Renaissance* 26 (1996): 423–50. The sources quoted are Heisch, "Queen Elizabeth I," 32; Montrose, "Elizabethan Subject," 310; and Frye, *Competition for Representation,* 54. For a brilliant analysis of the ways in which hasty assumptions about Elizabeth's sexuality have been made from misreadings and insufficient evidence, see John N. King, "Queen Elizabeth I: Representations of the Virgin Queen," *Renaissance Quarterly* 43 (spring 1990): 30–74.

13. See, for an exception, her French prayer, in Marcus, Mueller, and Rose, *Collected Works,* 314, where she thanks God for "[t]he honor of being mother and nurse of Thy dear children."

14. Mary Beth Rose, "Where Are the Mothers in Shakespeare?: Options for Gender Representation in the English Renaissance," *Shakespeare Quarterly* 42 (1991): 291–314.

15. Once again, versions of this argument are made in the sources listed in note 6. For an early version of the argument see Leah S. Marcus, "Shakespeare's Comic Heroines, Elizabeth I, and the Political Uses of Androgyny," in *Women in the Middle Ages and the Renaissance: Literary and Historical Perspectives,* ed. Mary Beth Rose (Syracuse, N.Y.: Syracuse University Press, 1986), 135–54.

16. Axton, *The Queen's Two Bodies,* 12. The classic study remains Ernst N. Kantorowicz, *The King's Two Bodies: A Study in Mediaeval Political Theory* (Princeton, N.J.: Princeton University Press, 1957).

17. See the brilliant analysis of Elizabeth's manipulations in this speech by Montrose in "Elizabethan Subject," 311–16.

18. Accounts of these incidents, events, and phenomena can be found in the many biographies of the queen, including (but by no means limited to) Perry, *Word of a Prince;* J. E. Neale, *Queen Elizabeth I: A Biography* (New York: Doubleday, 1957); Christopher Hibbert, *The Virgin Queen: Elizabeth I, Genius of the Golden Age* (Reading, Mass.: Addison-Wesley, 1991); Wallace MacCaffrey, *Elizabeth I* (London: Edward Arnold, 1993); Lacey Baldwin Smith, *Elizabeth Tudor: Portrait of a Queen* (Boston: Little, Brown, 1975); and my own personal favorite among recent biographies, Anne Somerset, *Elizabeth I* (New York: St. Martin's, 1991).

19. John Foxe, *Acts and Monuments of These Latter and Perilous Days* (London: John Day, 1563), 2096, 2097.

20. *The Political Works of James I,* ed. Charles Howard McIlwain (Cambridge, Mass.: Harvard University Press, 1918), 282.

21. Ibid., 282.

22. Jordan, *Renaissance Feminism*; Maureen Quilligan, *The Allegory of Female Authority: Christine de Pizan's Cité des Dames* (Ithaca: N.Y.: Cornell University Press, 1991).

23. I refer specifically to Marguerite de Navarre and Christine de Pizan. De Pizan's

Book of the City of Ladies (1403) was translated into English in the 1520s, although Elizabeth could undoubtedly have read it in the original French. Elizabeth also translated De Navarre's *Miroir de l'Ame Pecheresse* as a new year's gift for her stepmother, Katherine Parr (December 1544; see Marcus, Mueller, and Rose, *Collected Works,* 6). For an extremely insightful discussion of this translation (and particularly of some of Elizabeth's gendered choices), see Anne L. Prescott, "The Pearl of the Valois and Elizabeth I: Marguerite de Navarre's *Miroir* and Tudor England," in *Silent But For the Word: Tudor Women as Patrons, Translators, and Writers of Religious Works,* ed. Margaret Hannay (Kent, Ohio: Kent State University Press, 1985), 61–76.

24. Marguerite de Navarre, *The Heptameron,* trans. P. A. Chilton (London: Penguin, 1984), 61.

25. Christine de Pizan, *The Book of the City of Ladies,* trans. Earl Jeffrey Richards (New York: Persea, 1982), 4.

26. Quilligan, *Allegory of Female Authority,* 130–31, 79, 105.

27. De Pizan, *City of Ladies,* 4–5.

28. See, for example, John Stubbs, *Gaping Gulf,* ed. Lloyd E. Berry (Charlottesville: The Folger Shakespeare Library for the University Press of Virginia, 1968); and Philip Sidney, *Miscellaneous Prose,* ed. Katherine Duncan-Jones and Jan Van Dorsten (Oxford: Clarendon, 1973). Both Stubbs and Sidney wrote against Elizabeth's potential match with the Duke D'Alencon, the last of her courtships. Stubb's book was published, and he lost his right hand as a result, an order from the outraged queen. Sidney's letter circulated in manuscript and, although it has long been assumed that the queen virtually banished him from court as a result, Levin points out that, although Sidney did leave court, there is no real evidence for the assumption that the queen banished him (*Heart and Stomach of a King,* 62).

29. Elizabeth's possible fears of childbirth have also been noted by Levin, *Heart and Stomach of a King,* 86, and Haigh, *Elizabeth I: Profiles in Power* (London: Longman, 1988), 16. For discussions of deformed children, or what early modern Christians regarded as "monstrous births," see Retha M. Warnicke, *The Rise and Fall of Anne Boleyn* (Cambridge, Eng.: Cambridge University Press, 1989), 48–49; and Linda Charnes, *Notorious Identity: Materializing the Subject in Shakespeare* (Cambridge, Mass.: Harvard University Press, 1993), 22–28.

30. The best analysis of this phenomenon remains Montrose's brilliant "Shaping Fantasies: Figurations of Gender and Power in Elizabethan Culture," *Representations* 1 (spring 1983): 61–93. See also his "Celebration and Insinuation: Sir Philip Sidney and the Motives of Elizabethan Courtship," in *Renaissance Drama as Cultural History: Essays from Renaissance Drama,* ed. Mary Beth Rose (Evanston, Ill.: Northwestern University Press, 1990), 367–99; and Leonard Forster, "The Political Petrarchism of the Virgin Queen," in *The Icy Fire: Five Studies in European Petrarchism* (London: Cambridge University Press, 1969), 122–47.

31. Francis Bacon, "On the Fortunate Memory of Elizabeth Queen of England," *In Felicem Memoriam Elizabethae,* in *The Works of Francis Bacon,* ed. James Spedding et al. (Boston, 1860), 11: 460.

32. Neale, *Elizabeth I and Her Parliaments: 1559–1581,* 313–17; Heisch, "Queen Elizabeth I," 39.

33. Edward Hall, *Henry VIII* (London: T. C. and E. C. Jack, 1904), 2: 354–58.

34. McIlwain, *Political Works,* 318, 325.

35. Christopher Marlowe, *Tamburlaine the Great,* in *The Tudor Period,* vol. 1 of *Drama of the English Renaissance,* ed. Russell A. Fraser and Norman Rabkin (New York: Macmillan, 1976). For other salient examples of James's particular narcissism, see McIlwain, *Political Works,* 273, 328.

Chapter Three

1. See Catherine Gallagher, "Embracing the Absolute: The Politics of the Female Subject in Seventeenth-Century England," *Genders* 1 (March 1988): 24–39.

2. Margaret Cavendish, Duchess of Newcastle, *The Description of a New World, Called the Blazing-World* (London: A. Maxwell, 1668). All quotations from *Blazing-World* are cited in the text by page numbers.

3. See Natalie Zemon Davis, "Gender and Genre: Women as Historical Writers, 1400–1820," in *Beyond Their Sex: Learned Women of the European Past,* ed. Patricia H. Labalme (New York: New York University Press, 1980), and *Women on the Margins: Three Seventeenth-Century Lives* (Cambridge, Mass.: Harvard University Press, 1995). See also the introduction to Elspeth Graham, Hilary Hinds, Elaine Hobby, and Helen Wilcox, eds., *Her Own Life: Autobiographical Writings by Seventeenth-Century Englishwomen* (London: Routledge, 1989), 23: "For although the individual women may be 'unparalleled,' they are for the most part only able to define themselves by reference to the overpowering expectations and assumptions of womanhood made by seventeenth-century society."

For discussions of, and texts by, sectarian women, see Graham et al., *Her Own Life;* and Phyllis Mack, *Visionary Women: Ecstatic Prophecy in Seventeenth-Century England* (Berkeley: University of California Press, 1992).

4. Cf. Cynthia S. Pomerleau, "The Emergence of Women's Autobiography in England," in *Women's Autobiography: Essays in Criticism,* ed. Estelle C. Jelinek (Bloomington: Indiana University Press, 1980), 21–38. Pomerleau points out that "writings by women are among the early examples of the form" (22). Also see Sidonie Smith, *A Poetics of Women's Autobiography: Marginality and the Fictions of Self-Representation* (Bloomington: Indiana University Press, 1987), 42: "The very fact that women began writing autobiographies contemporary with the genre's emergence . . . is startling, disconcerting, and infinitely interesting."

5. See Lawrence Stone, *The Family, Sex, and Marriage in England 1500–1800* (New York: Harper and Row, 1977), 225–39; Margaret Bottrall, *Every Man a Phoenix: Studies in Seventeenth-Century Autobiography* (London: John Murray, 1958), 7–29; and Paul Delany, *British Autobiography in the Seventeenth Century* (London: Routledge and Kegan Paul, 1969), 11–12, 19.

For a critique of the ideology of the coherent self in its relation to English autobiography, see Felicity A. Nussbaum, *The Autobiographical Subject: Gender and Ideology in Eighteenth-Century England* (Baltimore: Johns Hopkins University Press, 1989), 25ff; Leigh Gilmore, *Autobiographics: A Feminist Theory of Women's Self-Representation* (Ithaca, N.Y.: Cornell University Press, 1994), xivff; and Smith, *Women's Autobiography,* 25–26.

6. Delany, *British Autobiography,* 22–23. Also see Jelinek, *Women's Autobiography,* 1–20; Judith Kegan Gardiner, "On Female Identity and Writing by Women," in *Writing and Sexual*

Difference, ed. Elizabeth Abel (Chicago: University of Chicago Press, 1980−82), 184−85; and Gilmore, *Autobiographics*, 14.

In *Every Man a Phoenix*, Bottrall points out that "oddly enough" the first extant English autobiography is written by a woman (1). She is referring, of course, to *The Book of Margery Kempe* (1438).

7. Delany, *British Autobiography*, 22−23; and Elizabeth W. Bruss, *Autobiographical Acts: The Changing Situation of a Literary Genre* (Baltimore: Johns Hopkins University Press, 1976), 7, 33.

8. Smith, *Women's Autobiography*, 14; and Graham et al., *Her Own Life*, 23.

9. Nussbaum, *Autobiographical Subject*, 24−25. See also Gilmore, *Autobiographics*, 14−15.

10. Georges Gusdorf, "Conditions and Limits of Autobiography," trans. James Olney, in *Autobiography: Essays Theoretical and Critical*, ed. James Olney (Princeton: Princeton University Press, 1980), 28−48.

11. Nussbaum, *Autobiographical Subject*, 27−28.

12. Ibid., 21.

13. All quotations are taken from Margaret Cavendish, Duchess of Newcastle, *A True Relation of My Birth, Breeding, and Life*, appended to *The Life of William Cavendish, Duke of Newcastle* (London: John C. Nimmo, 1886) and are cited in the text by page numbers.

14. Virginia Woolf, *Women and Writing*, ed. Michèle Barrett (New York: Harcourt Brace Jovanovich, 1979), 82. Judging as normative the male heroics of action, Woolf assumes the Marquis's defeats are the opposite of heroic. I argue in contrast that his military defeats are constitutive of (his) heroism.

15. Mary G. Mason, "The Other Voice: Autobiographies of Women Writers," in *Autobiography*, ed. James Olney, 207−35. In support of her point, Mason argues that Cavendish appended her own life story to her biography of her husband, *The Life of William Cavendish*, in 1667; but, as Mason concedes, *A True Relation* first appeared in 1656 as part of a miscellany of Cavendish's verse and prose, *Nature's Pictures Drawn by Fancies Pencil to the Life*, and can be considered a separate document. Cf. Smith, *Women's Autobiography*, 100.

16. Cf. Smith, who argues that in her autobiography Cavendish's husband "performs a function much like the woman 'in some corner' of Freud's male daydreams. He becomes a kind of male muse who acknowledges, who seems even to inspire, her writing" (*Women's Autobiography*, 97).

17. For two of many examples of Renaissance moral literature on the topic of gender ideology, see John Louis Vives, *Instruction of a Christian Woman*, trans. Richard Hyrde (London, 1557); and John Dod and Robert Cleaver, *A Godly Form of Household Government* (London, 1598). Also see Ian Maclean, *The Renaissance Notion of Woman* (Cambridge, Eng.: Cambridge University Press, 1980); Carroll Camden, *The Elizabethan Woman* (New York: Elsevier, 1952); Suzanne W. Hull, *Chaste, Silent, and Obedient: English Books for Women 1475−1640* (San Marino, Calif.: Huntington Library, 1982); and Ann Rosalind Jones, *The Currency of Eros: Women's Love Lyric in Europe, 1540−1620* (Bloomington: Indiana University Press, 1990), esp. 1−10.

18. Cf. Smith, who points to the use of heroic language in the quoted passage: "Ironi-

cally, while she means to mark the difference between herself and other women who use language publicly, the imagery in the passage identifies her with them. Like them, she would through writing enter the world of male combat and seek distinction on the field of battle. Like them, she seeks preeminence. That confusion in her recourse to the combat trope betrays the confusion at the heart of her project" (*Women's Autobiography,* 98).

19. Cavendish produced twenty-two folio volumes, including plays, poems, essays, sketches, philosophical treatises, and "orations of divers sorts." For a complete list of her works, see Douglas Grant, *Margaret the First: A Biography of Margaret Cavendish, Duchess of Newcastle 1623—1673* (London: Rupert Hart-Davis, 1957), 240—42.

20. All quotations are from John Loftis, ed., *The Memoirs of Anne, Lady Halkett and Ann, Lady Fanshawe* (Oxford: Clarendon, 1979), 101—92, and are cited in the text by page numbers. On 91—99 Loftis provides a textual history and chronology of the major events in Fanshawe's life.

21. Examples of the most popular literature expounding this ideal include Heinrich Bullinger, *The Golden Book of Christian Matrimony,* trans. Miles Coverdale (1543); William Perkins, *Christian Economy or Household Government* (1631); Dod and Cleaver, *A Godly Form of Household Government* (1598); Samuel Hieron, "The Marriage Blessing," in *The Sermons of Master Samuel Hieron* (1635); and William Gouge, *Of Domesticall Duties* (1622).

22. For a study of this narrative structure, see Northrop Frye, *The Secular Scripture: A Study of the Structure of Romance* (Cambridge, Mass.: Harvard University Press, 1976).

23. This distinction is made by Adrienne Rich in regard to motherhood in *Of Woman Born: Motherhood as Experience and Institution* (New York: Bantam, 1977).

24. All quotations are taken from Mrs. Alice Thornton, *Autobiography,* Surtees Society Publications, vol. 62 (London, 1873) and are cited in the text by page numbers.

25. See Stone, who reports that expectation of life in England in the 1640s was only thirty-two years, with newborn infants most at risk. Between a quarter and a third of all children of English peers and peasants were dead before they reached fifteen: "For women, childbirth was a very dangerous experience, for midwives were ignorant and ill-trained and often horribly botched the job, while the lack of hygienic precautions meant that puerperal fever was a frequent sequel" (*Family, Sex, and Marriage,* 68, 79).

26. Mason, "The Other Voice," 213. Cf. Wendy Martin, "Anne Bradstreet's Poetry: A Study of Subversive Piety," in *Shakespeare's Sisters: Feminist Essays on Women Poets,* ed. Sandra Gilbert and Susan Gubar (Bloomington: Indiana University Press, 1979), 21—22. Martin relates that, for Bradstreet, "suffering was a form of joy because the disaster that occasions it is a sign of God's love. . . . For the Puritans, affliction is a sign of the intimate bond between God and his children, it is not an indication of cruelty."

For harrowing accounts of the heroic suffering of female saints, see Caroline Walker Bynum, *Holy Feast and Holy Fast: The Religious Significance of Food to Medieval Women* (Berkeley: University of California Press, 1987).

27. See Peter Laslett, who reports that in late seventeenth-century England, "though so few people reached the age of seventy, it was regarded as the allotted span of life all the same" (*The World We Have Lost* [New York: Scribner's, 1965], 99).

28. See Stone, *Family, Sex, and Marriage,* 179—80; 270—81. Among the women under discussion, Anne Halkett is the best example of the "shift in basic attitude from deference to

autonomy" that Stone describes. Also see Mary, Countess of Warwick, *Autobiography*, ed. T. Crofton Croker, Percy Society Publications, vol. 22 (London, 1848), for another first-person account of a late-seventeenth-century woman who defied her father and married the man of her choice.

29. See Carol Gilligan, *In a Different Voice: Psychological Theory and Women's Development* (Cambridge, Mass.: Harvard University Press, 1982), 86.

30. All quotations from Anne Halkett are taken from Loftis, *Memoirs*, 9–87, and are cited in the text by page numbers. Loftis provides a textual history and chronology of the main events of Anne Halkett's life on 3–7.

31. See Teresa de Lauretis, *Alice Doesn't: Feminism, Semiotics, Cinema* (Bloomington: Indiana University Press, 1984). esp. 103–57; Mary Jacobus, *Reading Woman* (New York: Columbia University Press, 1984), 83–193; Gilligan, *In a Different Voice*; and Nancy Chodorow, *The Reproduction of Mothering: Psychoanalysis and the Sociology of Gender* (Berkeley: University of California Press, 1978). Also see Mary Beth Rose, "Where Are the Mothers in Shakespeare? Options for Gender Representation in the English Renaissance," *Shakespeare Quarterly* 42 (fall 1991): 291–314.

32. See Abel, *Writing and Sexual Difference*, in which many of the essays treat this issue. Also see Carolyn G. Heilbrun, *Reinventing Womanhood* (New York: Norton, 1979), 104–105, 124–97; and Lee R. Edwards, "The Labors of Psyche: Toward a Theory of Female Heroism," *Critical Inquiry* 6 (autumn 1979): 33–49.

33. Interestingly Loftis, the recent editor of Halkett's *Memoirs*, completely misses this point. Although he admires Halkett's intelligence, talent, and charm, he chooses to see her as a victim and her story as "a poignant account of humiliation and suffering" (xi). Thus, by choosing to pity her, Loftis unwittingly denies Halkett her dignity and power as an active protagonist in her own life.

34. There are several missing or mutilated leaves in the manuscript, which could shed further light on her mysterious relationship with C. B. My own guess is that they had a clandestine marriage, but it is only a guess.

35. Cf. Bottrall, *Every Man a Phoenix*, 11; and Keith Thomas, "Women and the Civil War Sects," *Past and Present* 13 (April, 1958): 42–52.

Chapter Four

1. For an analysis of the fortunes of the epic in its relation to politics and history during the Restoration, see Nigel Smith, *Literature and Revolution in England: 1640–1660* (New Haven, Yale University Press, 1994), especially chapter 7, 203–49. Arguing that the Civil War created a "process of transformation in which epic and heroic language was made to refer to inward states of human constitution and consciousness" (203), Smith traces the ways in which the epic's dialogue with history keeps changing epic structure and plot. He concludes that "The Civil War had proved the decadence of aristocratic martial, honour culture, and after 1660 traditional epic was no longer possible" (233).

All quotations from Milton's poetry are from Milton, *Complete Poems and Major Prose*, ed. Merritt Y. Hughes (Indianapolis: Odyssey, 1957) and are cited in the text by book and line numbers.

2. See Michael Wilding, *Dragon's Teeth: Literature in the English Revolution* (Oxford:

Clarendon, 1987), 173–204. Wilding comments (173) that "although past civil wars had later found epic treatment, the contemporary slaughter of fellow-countrymen could have little appeal." He goes on to demonstrate the antimilitary critique of traditional heroics in *Paradise Lost* and *Hudibras,* "the two most famous heroic poems of the Restoration."

3. Orlando Patterson, *Slavery and Social Death: A Comparative Study* (Cambridge, Mass.: Harvard University Press, 1982), 5. Also see William D. Phillips, Jr., *Slavery from Roman Times to the Early Transatlantic Slave Trade* (Minneapolis: University of Minnesota Press, 1985).

4. Mary Ann Radzinowicz, "The Distinctive Tragedy of *Samson Agonistes,*" *Milton Studies* 37 (1983): 249–50.

5. For an account of other seventeenth-century texts that, in contrast to Milton's play, do glorify Samson as a military hero, see Joseph Wittreich, *Interpreting Samson Agonistes* (Princeton: Princeton University Press, 1986), especially 103–5. Wittreich argues that Milton's play undertakes a reevaluation of heroism, but he (Wittreich) tends to define the heroic in moral terms: for example, "Milton's Samson is no villain, to be sure, but he *is* deeply flawed and thus ambiguous in his heroism" (italics in original). Also see John Steadman, *Milton and the Renaissance Hero* (Oxford: Clarendon, 1967), 27.

6. For an invaluable analysis of what he terms Milton's "theology of strength," see Michael Lieb, *The Sinews of Ulysses: Form and Convention in Milton's Works* (Pittsburgh: Duquesne University Press, 1989), 98–138. Lieb traces Milton's appropriation of the Old Testament tradition of conceptualizing strength as a manifestation of God's power and wisdom and the New Testament transvaluation of that concept into a paradoxical new form of strength as spiritual, rather than physical, and perfected in weakness: that is, in the patient endurance of affliction and suffering.

7. See Carole Pateman, *The Sexual Contract* (Stanford, Calif.: Stanford University Press, 1988), 120.

8. See Alan Sinfield, who provides a good assessment of the ways in which effeminacy in the Renaissance was connected not with male homoeroticism, but with heterosexuality and, particularly, with men who behaved or felt in what would normally be considered a "female" manner (*Cultural Politics—Queer Reading* [Philadelphia: University of Pennsylvania Press, 1994], 15).

9. Cf. Lieb, who observes, "Where Manoa errs, of course, is in assuming that the full return of strength can be realized without appropriate suffering." What Manoa offers is rest, but "it is indeed the rest of escape" (*Sinews of Ulysses,* 124).

10. See Wittreich, *Interpreting Samson Agonistes,* 62–80.

11. The bibliography on this subject has become extremely large. I offer only a few titles, many of which can lead the reader to other materials. While widely debated, Lawrence Stone's *The Family, Sex, and Marriage in England, 1500–1800* (New York: Harper and Row, 1977), remains invaluable. Also see Jack Goody, *The Development of the Family and Marriage in Europe* (Cambridge, Eng.: Cambridge University Press, 1983); Gordon J. Schochet, *Patriarchalism in Political Thought: The Authoritarian Family and Political Speculation and Attitudes, Especially in Seventeenth-Century England* (Oxford: Basil Blackwell, 1975); Margaret J. Ezell, *The Patriarch's Wife: Literary Evidence and the History of the Family* (Chapel Hill: University of North Carolina Press, 1987); Susan Dwyer Amussen, *An Ordered Society: Gender and Class in Early Modern England* (Oxford: Basil Blackwell, 1988), 314; and Frances E. Dolan, *Dangerous Fa-*

miliars: Representations of Domestic Crime in England, 1550—1700 (Ithaca, N.Y.: Cornell University Press, 1994).

12. Pateman, *Sexual Contract,* 90.

13. Alexander Niccholes, *A Discourse of Marriage and Wiving* (London, 1615), in *Harleian Miscellany,* vol. 2, ed. William Oldys, (1808—13), 162, 159, 164, 159, 161.

14. Mary Beth Rose, *The Expense of Spirit: Love and Sexuality in English Renaissance Drama* (Ithaca, N.Y.: Cornell University Press, 1988), 116—131, and "Where Are the Mothers in Shakespeare? Options for Gender Representation in the English Renaissance," *Shakespeare Quarterly* (fall 1991): 291—314.

15. William Whately, *A Care-cloth* (London, 1624), 33—34.

16. John Dod and Robert Cleaver, *A Godly Form of Household Government* (London, 1635), 149.

17. William Gouge, *Of Domesticall Duties* (London, 1622), 328.

18. See, for example, Gouge, *Domesticall Duties,* 295, 328; and Dod and Cleaver, *Household Government* (1635), sig. 06r.

19. Gouge, *Domesticall Duties,* 356.

20. Cf. John Guillory, "Dalila's House: *Samson Agonistes* and the Sexual Division of Labor," in *Rewriting the Renaissance: The Discourses of Sexual Difference in Early Modern Europe,* ed. Margaret W. Ferguson, Maureen Quilligan, and Nancy Vickers (Chicago: University of Chicago Press, 1986), 106—22, and "The Father's House: *Samson Agonistes* in Its Historical Moment," in *Re-Membering Milton: Essays on the Texts and Traditions,* ed. Mary Nyquist and Margaret W. Ferguson (New York: Methuen, 1987), 148—76.

21. Thomas Hobbes, *Leviathan,* ed. Michael Oakeshott (New York: Macmillan, 1962), 152—53.

22. John Locke, *The Second Treatise of Civil Government,* in *Two Treatises of Government,* ed. Thomas I. Cook (New York: Hafner, 1947), 161

23. See, for example, Gouge, *Domesticall Duties,* 241; and Whately, *Care-cloth,* 80—82.

24. Michael Lieb, *Milton and the Culture of Violence* (Ithaca, N.Y.: Cornell University Press, 1994), 260.

25. Cf. Jackie DiSalvo, "Intestine Thorn: Samson's Struggle with the Woman Within," in *Milton and the Idea of Woman,* ed. Julia Walker (Urbana: University of Illinois Press, 1988), 211—29.

26. Cf. *Paradise Regained,* the companion text to *Samson Agonistes,* in which Christ unproblematically inhabits the position of female hero, defined by his absolute resistance to being seduced. In further contrast, Christ ends by peacefully (unambivalently) returning home to his mother's house, although we know he will not remain there.

27. Locke, *Second Treatise,* 133.

28. Cf. Rose, *Expense of Spirit,* 93—127, for a relevant discussion of the fates of Zenocrate in Marlowe's *Tamburlaine,* Shakespeare's Desdemona, and Webster's Duchess of Malfi.

29. See Laura Brown, "The Romance of Empire: *Oroonoko* and the Trade in Slaves," in *The New Eighteenth Century: Theory, Politics, English Literature,* ed. Felicity Nussbaum and Laura Brown (New York: Methuen, 1987), 41—61; and Moira Ferguson, *Subject to Others: British Women Writers and Colonial Slavery, 1670—1834* (New York: Routledge, 1992), 3—49.

30. All quotations from *Oroonoko* are taken from the edition edited by Lore Metzger (New York: Norton, 1973) and are cited in the text by page number.

31. Laura J. Rosenthal, "Owning Oroonoko: Behn, Southerne, and the Contingencies of Property," in *Renaissance Drama* n.s. 23 (1992): 25–58.

32. For essays that deal with the complexities of the relation of skin color to conceptions of race in the early modern period, see *Women, 'Race,' and Writing in the Early Modern Period*, ed. Margo Hendricks and Patricia Parker (London: Routledge, 1994), and two essays in *Renaissance Drama* n.s. 23 by Kim F. Hall, "Guess Who's Coming to Dinner? Colonization and Miscegenation in *The Merchant of Venice*," 87–111, and Margo Hendricks, "Managing the Barbarian: *The Tragedy of Dido, Queen of Carthage*," 165–88.

33. Margaret Ferguson, "News from the New World: Miscegenous Romance in Aphra Behn's *Oroonoko* and *The Widow Ranter*," in *The Production of English Renaissance Culture*, ed. David Lee Miller, Sharon O'Dair, and Harold Weber (Ithaca, N.Y.: Cornell University Press, 1994), 151–89. Cf. her "Juggling the Categories of Race, Class, and Gender: Aphra Behn's *Oroonoko*," in *Women, 'Race,' and Writing*, ed. Hendricks and Parker, 209–24, and "Transmuting *Othello*: Aphra Behn's *Oroonoko*," in *Cross-Cultural Performances: Differences in Women's Re-Visions of Shakespeare*, ed. Marianne Novy (Urbana: University of Illinois Press, 1993), 15–49. For further valuable discussion of the ideological complexity of the text, see Brown, "Romance of Empire"; and Moira Ferguson, *Subject to Others*, 27–49.

34. For a brilliant analysis of Oroonoko's vulnerability to being entertained, see Robert L. Chibka, "'Oh! Do Not Fear a Woman's Invention': Truth, Falsehood, and Fiction in Aphra Behn's *Oroonoko*," in *Texas Studies in Literature and Language* 30, no. 4 (winter 1988): 510–37.

35. For further discussion of this point, see Moira Ferguson, *Subject to Others*, 40–45.

36. Pateman, *Sexual Contract*, 60.

37. Cf. Margaret Ferguson, "Juggling," 214–15, where she traces the narrator's inconsistent use of personal pronouns when she (the narrator) uneasily seeks to identify herself both with the slaves and the colonialists.

38. Patterson, *Slavery and Social Death*, 13. See also Phillips, *Slavery from Roman Times*, 6–14.

39. Charlotte Sussman, "The Other Problem with Women: Reproduction and Slave Culture in Aphra Behn's *Oroonoko*," in *Rereading Aphra Behn: History, Theory, and Criticism*, ed. Heidi Hutner (Charlottesville: University Press of Virginia, 1993), 212–33. The quotation is on page 220.

40. See Margaret Ferguson, "Juggling," and "Transmuting *Othello*," 35; and Sussman, "The Other Problem with Women," 212–33. I am also grateful to Carolyn Swift, who was the first to point out to me the importance of the fact that Imoinda wounds the governor.

41. See Locke, *Second Treatise*, 161–63.

42. All quotations are from Mary Astell, *Some Reflections upon Marriage, Occasion'd by the Duke and Dutchess of Mazarine's Case; which is also consider'd*. 2d ed. (London: Printed for R. Wilkin, at the King's Head in St. Paul's Church-Yard, 1703) and are cited in the text by page number.

43. For astute analyses of the contradictions between and among Astell's feminism and her political and religious conservatism, see Ruth Perry, *The Celebrated Mary Astell: An Early*

English Feminist (Chicago: University of Chicago Press, 1986), 150–69; and Catherine Gallagher, "Embracing the Absolute: The Politics of the Female Subject in Seventeenth Century England," *Genders* 1 (March 1988): 24–39.

Epilogue

1. Northrop Frye, *Anatomy of Criticism: Four Essays* (Princeton: Princeton University Press, 1957), 37.

2. The classic statement of this position in Renaissance studies is Joan Kelly's essay, "Did Women Have a Renaissance?" in *Women, History and Theory: The Essays of Joan Kelly* (Chicago: University of Chicago Press, 1984), 19–50.

Index